WHAT'S THE PO!NT

MICAEL DAHLEN

WHAT'S THE PO!NT

HOW TO FIND MEANING IN YOUR LIFE

A LITTLE BOOK ABOUT A BIG QUESTION

Volante

What's the Point : How to Find Meaning in Your Life

Volante
Stora Nygatan 7
111 27 Stockholm
www.volante.se

Original title: En liten bok om meningen med livet
Translation: Elizabeth DeNoma
Cover and inlay: Miroslav Sokcic
ISBN: 978-91-7965-386-6

TABLE OF CONTENTS

PREFACE

THIS IS a little book about a very big question, maybe the most important question of them all. It contains what I know for sure about how a person can feel that their life is meaningful, results from my own research and that of others. And that's obviously/demonstrably not too much. Because for all that people have been pondering over the meaning of life for thousands of years, it's only in recent years that we have started to research what gives people meaning in their lives.

Maybe we're living in a time when we need this more than ever before. To have a sense of meaning in our lives, that is, not this book. But if the little I've learned can help just a little, I'll be very happy. When you're feeling a little lost or you're brooding. When you're looking for something more. Or if only to discover that you're not alone, because I'm lost too, brooding and searching. Then this book will have done its work.

I hope it can make you a little happy, too, with some of my quirky stories. And that it might give you a reason to talk about life, your life, with someone for a while. To share it and discover together the amazing life we have.

WHAT'S THE POINT?

DO YOU KNOW what the meaning of life is?

Maybe that's a dumb question. After all, it has been twisted and turned over one way and another for thousands of years, by various religions, philosophies, biology, and cosmology, and still there is no clear-cut answer.

Maybe the meaning of life is to serve God, to get to heaven, Nirvana, oneness, or whatever the final destination is, the one where we reach ultimate enlightenment or are freed from all forms of suffering? It depends a little on whether you ask Islam, Judaism, Christianity, Buddhism, or Hinduism. Or maybe the meaning of life is to attain the highest level of knowledge, as Plato proposed, to do the highest good, as Aristotle believed, to endure, which is the overall solution to life according to Stoicism, or any of the other answers offered by the many *isms* of Greek philosophy. Alternately, the Enlightenment philosopher Immanuel Kant would say that the meaning of life is to do one's moral duty, and the 19th century philosopher Friedrich Nietzsche would say that life, in fact, has no meaning at all. There are probably as many answers as there are philosophers (that is also a very difficult question to answer: how many philosophers are there in the history of the world?).

The world's most famous biologist, Charles Darwin, argued that the point of life is to survive (which seems a bit like a circular argument?) while the world's second most famous biologist, with the confusingly similar name of Richard Dawkins, believes that life is about reproducing (or more specifically, replicating one's genes). If your head isn't sufficiently spinning by now, try asking biologists what constitutes life (the jury is still out, if I can put it that way...).

The physicists conclude simply that we have too little evidence to even make an educated guess—human life has only existed, as far as we know, for 0.04% of the almost 14-billion-year history of the cosmos (if we include the first amoebae, this increases to a few tenths of a percent) and on a single planet, or 0.0000006% of all the planets in our galaxy.

In 2020, some researchers at Cornell University published a scientific paper concluding that there might actually be a total of 26 civilizations in different parts of our galaxy, but that remains to be seen. Their discouraging conclusion is that humanity will probably die out before we have time to make contact with any of them (so our chances of learning if they found any point in existence must be considered futile). It was therefore Stephen Hawking's conclusion that the purpose of life is to study the universe, while Einstein argued that the meaning of life is an illusion, but a necessary one.

Maybe Einstein's answer points to why the question has been with us throughout time: because we don't know the answer but need to believe that one actually exists.

Maybe that's why the search term phrase "the meaning of life" returns over a billion results on Google (which places it near the top of the list statistically, not too far after number one, "weather forecast?") Speaking of the weather, I tested my own hypothesis and found that internet searches on the meaning of life are most frequent during the darkest and coldest months of the year (with the exception of holidays like Christmas and New Year's). That's when many people find life to be at its most weighty (I've even found that in my own happiness research: average happiness is lowest in winter, especially in February, which is the coldest and most illness-ridden month of the year. This also led me to correlate meaning-of-life searches with searches for illness; the results are the same pattern).

I also cross-referenced the results and found that searches on the meaning of life go up at the same time as searches for "economy." (With the exception of economics professors, people really only search for topics related to the economy when it's something they are worried about.) Same thing with unemployment and divorce.

People all over the world are pondering the meaning of life, whether they live in Australia, Sweden, Azerbaijan, or Zimbabwe. Over 60% said they do so *often* or *sometimes* in a survey conducted a year or so ago among some 100,000 people in 80 different countries.

Whatever the meaning of life is, we all seem to need one. To lean on it sometimes, perhaps most of all when life is difficult or takes an unexpected turn. Perhaps we need it now more than ever, with all the information flooding in and it becoming increasingly difficult to know what is true or "true." With all the choices we have to make and all the different roads we can choose between in life, and with the global pandemic that shut down nearly the entire world, making us realize that we really can't take anything for granted. When I asked more than 1,000 Swedes a few months into the COVID-19 pandemic, 38% said they were thinking more about the meaning of life, and almost half thought the question had become more important.

Curiously, there has been very little research, and indeed no studies at all, on what the meaning of life is. Philosophers, as we have seen, have always wrestled with the question, but it is as if the subject is too elusive for science. But it can be reformulated.

So let me ask you a new question: Do you feel that your life has meaning?

This question is actually not nearly as dumb as the first one. It hasn't been turned over for thousands of years; in fact it's probably only been asked for just more than 60 years, since 1959, when the Austrian psychotherapist Viktor Frankl summarized his experiences of surviving the concentration camps during the Second World War in the book *Man's Search for Meaning.* In it he laid the foundations for logotherapy, which translates to "meaning therapy." Logotherapy is considered one of the three classic Austrian psychotherapy theories, along with Freud's psychoanalysis and Adler's inferiority complex.

From the 1960s onwards, a number of new fields of research developed that have approached the question from different perspectives, such as the theory of existentialism, meaning processing, fear management, psychological well-being, purposefulness, life reflection, flourishing, life narratives, and meaning of life. So now there have been several thousand studies. And hundreds of thousands of people all over the world have answered the question unequivocally in the form of a yes or no, or on a scale from, say, 1 to 10. Canadians, Kenyans and Chinese, Hungarians and Uzbeks, Swedes and Americans. Young and old, schoolchildren, and prison inmates. The question comes in several forms, some variants consisting of up to 40 sub-questions (psychotherapists and psychologists are *very* fond of asking things in various ways) but comparative studies show that it doesn't really matter which variant is used; the answer to the question is broadly the same.

So on a scale of 1 to 10, how would you answer?

1 2 3 4 5 6 7 8 9 10

I don't dare hazard a guess as to which number you dialed. If the question had been about happiness, I'd be pretty sure you'd be a bit on the upper half of the scale, because most people are. But feeling that one's life is meaningful is not the same as feeling happiness.

A happy life is not necessarily a meaningful life (researchers at Ohio State University found that three out of four people agreed with that statement). And feeling that one's life is meaningful doesn't have to make you happy (two out of three agreed with that, too). In fact, feeling that one's life is meaningful can, in some ways, be an alternative to happiness, something that gets you up in the morning (even in February) and gets you through the day when happiness is the last thing that you're feeling. That helps you feel hope instead of confusion, helps you to undertake challenges and deal with setbacks.

Studies have shown that having a feeling of meaning in one's life has a great number of important effects on our well-being. It makes us more optimistic, helps us cope with stress and sadness, helps us sleep better, and reduces our risk of depression. It also reduces our risk of going to prison (or helps you put up with prison, if you're already in there) or addiction (and helps in kicking addiction, if you already have one) and makes you play hooky less and read more (if you go to school, that is, at least that's what the Organisation for Economic Co-operation and Development (OECD) found in a study of over half a million 15-year-olds throughout 79 countries). A sense of purpose in life also helps you live longer, both by reducing risky behaviors such as getting into fights and conflicts or wanting to commit suicide, and by boosting your immune system, keeping your blood pressure low, and maintaining the health of your heart, liver, and other vital organs.

Studies that have followed thousands of people over several

years, such as American retirees, middle-aged Britons and Germans in their 20s and 80s, have found that those who feel a greater sense of purpose in their lives are between 10 and 30% more likely to still be alive the next time the researchers come looking for them. If nothing else, a sense of purpose makes life less boring at a minimum and probably even more long-lasting (yes, there are studies on that too).

Regardless of where you find yourself on the scale, I hope that this book can help you land a little higher up on it and feel a little better. It won't give you the definitive answer to the meaning of life (which is hardly surprising at this point) or even the answer to how you can, once and for all, experience more meaning in your life. But the following chapters contain a bunch of tips that you can use in different situations when life requires a little more meaning, to give yourself a little boost up on the scale. All the tips are based on existing research in this surprisingly novel and unexplored area. To find them, I really had to search, because it seems that it hasn't occurred to us scientists until recently that we should look a little more closely at what makes people feel as though their lives are meaningful. But the tips and advice I'm highlighting are ones that have been proven to work.

I'm going to borrow from all those fields of research that have emerged over the last 60 years and you'll see that the various religions, philosophers, biologists, and cosmologists have really useable points. I've also cherry-picked the most useful answers people themselves have given to the question of what gives meaning to their lives (there have been several, as these kinds of surveys from around the world and their results are quite similar). And of course I'll share with you several of my own studies.

So here we go.

What can you do to feel that your life is a little more meaningful?

»BUT FEELING THAT ONE'S LIFE IS MEANINGFUL IS NOT THE SAME AS FEELING HAPPINESS. A HAPPY LIFE IS NOT NECESSARILY A MEANINGFUL LIFE (RESEARCHERS AT OHIO STATE UNIVERSITY FOUND THAT THREE OUT OF FOUR PEOPLE AGREED WITH THAT STATEMENT). AND FEELING THAT ONE'S LIFE IS MEANINGFUL DOESN'T HAVE TO MAKE YOU HAPPY (TWO OUT OF THREE AGREED WITH THAT, TOO). IN FACT, FEELING THAT ONE'S LIFE IS MEANINGFUL CAN, IN SOME WAYS, BE AN ALTERNATIVE TO HAPPINESS, SOMETHING THAT GETS YOU UP IN THE MORNING (EVEN IN FEBRUARY) AND THAT GETS YOU THROUGH THE DAY WHEN HAPPINESS IS THE LAST THING THAT YOU'RE FEELING...«

THINK ABOUT DEATH!

MEMENTO MORI. Roman generals had a tradition to parade the capital after major war victories. The parade would make its way through the entire city of Rome and could last an entire day. Standing behind the general on the chariot this whole time would be a slave, whispering in his ear, "remember that you are mortal". I came to think of that tradition when I heard the ice cream truck outside my window the other day. Maybe it would be a good idea to have a truck driving through the neighborhood once a week or so, trumpeting "think about death!" out of its little speaker on the roof?

According to existential theory, death is one of the four ultimate human dilemmas that drive us to seek meaning in life (more on the others in later chapters). Socrates even argued that this is why we have philosophy, to think and find meaning in the face of death. The Buddhists meditate on it in their *maranasati*, which means "awareness of death" and is the most elevated form of meditation that allows death to shed light on life.

There have been a lot of studies on near-death experiences, so many in fact that there is a special scientific journal devoted to them, with the telling name *Journal of Near-Death Studies* (not to be confused with the journal *Death Studies*, for studies on less fortunate outcomes). The studies show that near-death experiences can be very traumatic on the one hand, but that they can also be positive in the long run.

In one such study, doctors interviewed all heart attack patients hospitalized in the US city of St. Louis over a three-year period and found that their near-death experiences were often about what they had and had not done in their lives. In a follow-up six months later, the patients reported feeling significantly more meaning in their lives.

Another study compared students who had near-death experiences, such as a car accident or near-drowning, with those who had not come close to death in the same way and found that they were on average three steps higher on that scale you were asked to place yourself on in the introduction to the book.

Interviews with people related to someone who has died show that as their grief begins to subside, more and more of those people also began to look for and experience greater meaning in their own lives.

For me, everything changed after a phone call from my father. He had asked me out to lunch a month earlier. I think it was actually the first time we met for lunch in the city and I was naturally curious about the reason. It turned out to be that he had decided to take early retirement. He had worked long enough, he said. His situation was such that he and his wife could get by on what they had, and now it was time to live. And time for the two of us to really get to know each other.

I'm not sure if he said that last part or if I just thought it, but it's my strongest memory of the lunch. I grew up with my mom and saw my dad one weekend a month; they were divorced and he worked a lot. I was really looking forward to him stopping that and to all the time we would now have together. But when Dad called a month later, it wasn't to tell me he'd stopped working, but to tell me that the reason he'd been so tired lately turned out to be that he had blood cancer. A very rare form that the doctors didn't know much about and couldn't cure. It was impossible to know how much time he had left. This made me see my own life in a whole new light, that life I had dedicated to working and achieving, just like him—perhaps partly for that very reason, to show that I could do that, too. That life that I would live for real, just like him.

What if there is no later?

After that conversation I started painting my fingernails black, as a reminder to myself to be who I am, not to hide (at that time it was quite difficult not to stand out as a man with painted nails) and to live my life now that I can, whatever it is.

My advice to you is to do the same. Not necessarily paint your fingernails black (but that's actually really cool-looking, I think), but to remind yourself that there may not be a later. Kind of like that expression, "One day we're all going to die. Every other day we're not going to."

One day you're going to die, but what are you going to do with the other days?

Research in fear management shows that even small reminders of death can be enough to make people see the meaning of life in a stronger light. For example, researchers have tried treating people with mild depression by asking them to think about their own death and found that it increased their sense of meaning in life (though whether they became less depressed wasn't included in the study).

A German research team stopped people in the street 100 meters before or after they passed a funeral home and asked them about current public and personal events, reporting that those who had passed the funeral home ranked the events as more significant. When American researchers repeated the field study, they got the same results.

There are a whole bunch of studies that remind people in different ways of death to see how that influences their experience of meaning in their lives. For example, by having people read scenarios about waking up in the morning and inhaling the scent of either freshly brewed coffee or the smell of smoke in their home. Those people who imagined the smell of smoke would mark themselves a little higher on the self-evaluation scale.

In other experiments, researchers have asked people to write down what they think will happen when they die, and compared their answers to those of people who'd been asked to think about something that is also traumatic but that doesn't bring to mind death, like a dental visit (for myself, having grown up with a dentist mother, I'll have to take the researchers' word for it; I remember it as being very boring) or an exam (which students apparently find almost as traumatic). The researchers found a similar result—that those who wrote about death scored higher on the meaning-in-their-life scale and saw greater value in past events in their lives. People have also been asked to solve crosswords containing words that are supposed to remind them of death (words like *funeral*) or completely random words like *lamp*, with the same results.

Despite painting my nails black for many years now, ever since that phone call from my dad, I was affected by the reports of disaster and the death toll during the pandemic. The abstract death reflected in my nails became very obtrusive and tangible again.

I sat down to search for studies that more closely examined whether the coronavirus made people more sensitized to the meaning in their lives. It turned out that other researchers had been wondering along the same lines during times of earlier catastrophes. Three months after 9/11 researchers interviewed American students and found that they valued their lives more highly and ascribed greater meaning to them.

A few years later, another team of researchers conducted random telephone interviews with people of all ages in Hong Kong in the midst of the SARS epidemic and reported similar results. However, there were no studies on the coronavirus yet.

So, I conducted one myself. I asked 1,000 Swedes and found that almost half felt they attached greater importance to the meaning of their lives since the coronavirus outbreak.

In the midst of all the horror and terror, at least the pandemic had a positive effect on how many of us value our lives and their meaning. The only real question is how long that will last. After all, we have a tendency to forget, not least of all about our mortality, which we are happy to repress even when it's there painted in black on our fingernails. I don't think American students would give the same answer today as they did in the 2001 interviews. The Hong Kong researchers could see how people responded differently just four months after the SARS epidemic.

Thinking about death is creepy and difficult. But maybe if we do it a little more often, it will get easier?

Start each day with the thought "One day I will die. But what should I do today?" and make the day more vibrant and meaningful. Or imagine a car pulling into your street every two weeks or so trumpeting "Think about death!" out of a little speaker on the roof.

It doesn't feel like a particularly cheery tip. That's why I chose to start the book with it, so that it's out of the way. Because death is really the most life-affirming thing there is, a reminder that life is absolutely amazing and that it's yours to live right now.

»DEATH IS REALLY THE MOST LIFE-AFFIRMING THING THERE IS, A REMINDER THAT LIFE IS ABSOLUTELY AMAZING AND THAT IT'S YOURS TO LIVE RIGHT NOW.«

NATUREWATCH!

TEN YEARS after Viktor Frankl released his groundbreaking book on man's search for meaning in life, a study conducted in 1969 found that more than half of Inuit schoolchildren in the northern tip of Alaska were nearsighted. By contrast, among their grandparents, who hadn't gone to school in their youth, only two of the 131 still alive were found to be nearsighted.

The researchers concluded that reading books at school was probably the culprit, an idea put forward by the German astronomer Johannes Kepler—both a leading figure in the scientific revolution and someone who was myopic—back in the 17th century (this was followed by the suggestion that school desks should have stands to rest students' heads on to make reading less taxing).

Now you, who are evidently reading a book right now, might be worried. But don't worry, you don't have to put this book down. Johannes Kepler was right about many things, such as how celestial bodies move in the universe, but he was wrong about reading. Reading won't make you nearsighted. That's what the highly regarded scientific journal *Nature* noted recently in a review of all studies done since 1969 that found and tried to explain why myopia has doubled over time in Europe and the US, rising from around 25% to over 80% among twentysomethings in countries like Singapore, South Korea and Taiwan.

The reason turned out to be—not increased time in front of books and screens—but time spent indoors. The explains why Australian youth, who according to statistics, spend significantly more time outdoors, have not had nearly the same kinds of increased myopia and why experiments in China, for example, where parts of the school day have been moved outdoors, reduced children's propensity to become myopic by about half. This is because outdoors the light is more natural (which affects biochemistry in the eye) and the distance to the horizon is longer, which trains the eye's perspective vision.

So spending time outdoors in nature makes you less nearsighted and gives you greater perspective. Both literally and figuratively, as we shall see in this chapter.

That's why my advice is to naturewatch.

For example, you can look at moss. Moss-watching actually has become popular in Japan in recent years. It has become a trend especially among young women to go on "moss weekends" and organize moss parties and share moss-related pictures and ideas on Pinterest to unwind and get away from everyday problems. Whether that makes their lives feel more meaningful doesn't come up; no one seems to have thought to ask.

But for the Japanese, nature has been a religion for 2,000 years. According to Shintoism, which the majority of Japanese adhere to, humanity and nature are a single entity and life is about reverence for nature. Unlike many of the other major religions, Shintoism doesn't have any temples but has instead sacred sites within nature, such as Mount Fuji. These same religious ideas about the meaning of life being found in nature can be found throughout the world, among the Sámi, Pygmies, and Inuits, for example (at least among the less myopic grandparents).

Even Enlightenment philosopher Jean-Jacques Rousseau, who many believe helped lay the foundations of modern Western societies with his ideas that inspired both the French and American revolutions (and education), landed eventually in his old age on the idea that the meaning of life is to live simply and close to nature.

And while no one thought to ask the trendy young moss-watchers in Japan, researchers studying meaning in life have asked Americans, Britons, Chinese, Germans and New Zealanders, among others, whether they experience it in nature. Almost half of the 5,000 Americans surveyed agreed that nature gives meaning in life, over half of New Zealanders spontaneously mentioned nature in response to the question, and among Germans, most thought it was important, with people over 70 even considering nature to be one of the most important sources of meaning in their lives. Researchers have also asked students to take photos of things they find meaningful in life and found that nature motifs such as mountains, rivers, landscapes, and seasons were among the most common images.

One explanation for why nature makes people experience more meaning in their lives is that it broadens our myopic perspective out from the short time we humans are on earth. Physicists love to point out that humanity's history makes up a fraction of a decimal point in the history of the universe, compared to the larger perspective of billions of years that the mountains, rivers, and landscapes we find ourselves in have existed. Nature reminds us of our part in a larger cycle.

Scientists have conducted a range of experiments in which people have been asked to imagine themselves out in nature or indoors, to look at pictures of a natural or indoor environment, or to take a short walk along a small tree-lined river or corridor.

In all cases, those who had been in contact with nature in some way reported feeling more alive.

The researchers also tried asking subjects at random times of the day to report how alive they felt and found that those who were in an outdoor environment at the time scored higher on the scale, whether they were in Canada or Germany, where the experiments were conducted.

Subjects who were in Ann Arbor, Michigan were found to be better at memorizing and reciting syllables backwards when American researchers sent them on a walk through the city's public park, compared to those who were instead given a walk through the downtown neighborhoods. Nature literally cleared their heads of distracting thoughts. When the researchers repeated the experiment on mildly depressed people, they got the same results and found that nature made them brood and fret less, and look less negatively at past events in their lives. Accordingly my advice is to get out in nature a little bit every day and be a little less myopic. Clear your head of distressing and negative thoughts; feel the closeness to nature and life. As a bonus you'll be a whiz at rattling off a series of numbers backwards (and won't have to think about getting a headrest to use when you're reading books or limiting screen time to save your eyes).

Just go to a park or some small green space in town. But it's best to get out of the city and into the woods, mountains, or a body of water, as British researchers found in a comparison. Is 15 minutes a day enough, you might ask? (If you didn't before, you probably are now that I'm asking).

No, when the researchers compared people who were encouraged to go out into nature every day for 30 days, they found that only those who were outside for at least 30 minutes experienced clear increases on the self-reported scale of meaning in their lives.

If you don't have 30 minutes to spend in nature (perhaps it's time to reassess the business of your life?), take a quick photo of it. "Take a picture, it'll last longer," as the Yanks say. Anyway, those American researchers (who found that people often took photos of nature when asked to take pictures of things that gave meaning to their lives) did a follow-up study where they found that the photography itself also increased a sense of meaning in life. When they asked subjects to take photos of things and moments that gave their lives meaning, the subjects scored higher on the meaning scale afterwards.

You might be thinking that soon there may be no nature left to photograph. Maybe you're more likely to think that if you're Swedish (we have the highest climate awareness in Europe according to EU statistics, anyway). So you have twice as much reason to save it. Not only does nature itself, for as long as it lasts, increase our sense of meaning in our lives, saving/preserving nature also gives us greater meaning. A study of nearly 300 Swedish 12-year-olds found that those who believed the climate was under threat felt greater purpose in their lives, and a complementary survey of just under 300 Swedish teenagers found that those who were involved in protecting/saving/preserving the climate in various ways also scored higher on the meaning scale.

I couldn't find a study on adults, so I did my own on 600 people between 18 and 86. The correlation turns out to apply to all of us. Regardless of age, people who thought the climate issue was important, and who were hopeful about solving it, felt more meaning in their lives (while those who were pessimistic felt, instead, less meaning).

So please, for the sake of the planet, for all of us, and for your own sake: help protect nature and the climate.

And for my sake: go out and look at some moss and tell me if it gives you more meaning in life (I can't bear to leave that question unanswered).

»ONE EXPLANATION FOR WHY NATURE GIVES PEOPLE A GREATER SENSE OF PURPOSE IN LIFE IS THAT IT BROADENS THE MYOPIC PERSPECTIVE FROM THE SHORT TIME WE ARE ON EARTH, TO THE LARGER PERSPECTIVE OF BILLIONS OF YEARS THAT THE MOUNTAINS, RIVERS, AND LANDSCAPES IN WHICH WE LIVE HAVE EXISTED. NATURE REMINDS US OF OUR PART IN A BIGGER CYCLE OF THINGS.«

TEMPLE!
(A VERB)

ICELANDERS ARE the fittest people in the world. There are actually statistics that prove it. Not only have they popped out female CrossFit finalists and World's Strongest Man winners through the years like no other country has. Almost all of its more than 300,000 inhabitants work out regularly, young and old. They exercise more on average each week than people in any other country. Maybe that's why Icelanders also live longer than almost everyone else. According to UN statistics, in 2020 they were eighth out of all the countries in the world, to be precise. And maybe that's why they endure the cold, harsh climate in the dark on a tiny island in the middle of the North Atlantic (for me that's always been a mystery; it's like almost all their year is a long, horrible February) for their entire long lives?

Because exercise can give life a little more meaning.

"There's no reason to be alive if you can't deadlift," said Jon Pall Sigmarsson, who won the World's Strongest Man competition no fewer than four times. He's probably the only one who feels that way (myself, I feel mostly anxiety when it comes to my own deadlift sessions). But most people seem to agree at least that being fit and healthy makes life more meaningful.

When researchers asked 5,000 Americans what makes their life meaningful, almost one in five people said good health and fitness, more than twice as many as those who said doing good or making a difference. Being healthy and feeling good (fifth place) was also a more common response than doing good deeds for the more than 30,000 people who filled out the Church of Sweden's online survey about the meaning of life. (What was the very surprising first place? Riding a motorcycle. I'll come back to that later.)

The idea that a healthy life is a meaningful life is also to be found in both religion and philosophy. Take the Bible, for example, from which the expression "your body is a temple" is taken. Man is made in God's image, and to take care of one's body is to honor God. Anyone who has seen the painting *The Creation of Adam* (also known as *The Finger of God*) in the Sistine Chapel, which is perhaps the most famous Christian depiction of God, realizes that it takes a lot of training to get a torso as muscular as portrayed there.

The same is true if you want to look like a Roman statue. The Romans coined the phrase *mens sana in corpore sano*, which means "a healthy mind in a healthy body." Half a millennium earlier, the Greek philosopher Thales was already on the same track when he argued that happiness comes from a healthy body (along with a calm mind).

That's why my advice is to *temple*—nurture and build your body as if it were a temple. In fact, your body can literally be your temple, allowing you to live longer and better and fill your life with more meaning. A strong and healthy body makes it easier to get out into nature. It gives you strength, energy, and actually makes it easier to follow all the other tips to come in this book in order to feel more purpose and pleasure in your life.

Exercise a little more and you'll soon notice the difference yourself. If you're like most people, you already wish you did. Three out of four said they would like to exercise more than they do when I asked 1,000 randomly selected Swedes. Now you have a much better reason to do it than that it was a New Year's resolution (which is 50% likely to be broken before the end of January; yeah, I did a study on that, too) or that you want to fit better in your swimwear for the summer—namely that it actually makes your life feel a little more meaningful.

This has been shown to be true for everyone from South African gym-goers to British 86- to 99-year-olds. Studies have been done on both groups, showing how they experienced increased meaning in their lives as they got into the habit of working out. The same goes for Koreans, Finnish pensioners, cancer patients, and people with Parkinson's disease.

Exercise, whether it's lifting weights, running, cycling, walking with poles or water aerobics, gives purpose and meaning to life, the research shows. The same goes for kettlebell training, I'm guessing.

Sales of kettlebells in the US certainly increased by 600%

in the first few months of the pandemic. The same goes for other forms of exercise equipment, which increased by hundreds of percent on Amazon and Walmart, and other retailers. Of course, this could be because people needed equipment to work out at home instead of at the gym during the quarantine (which would also explain why sales of upper body clothes increased but not lower body clothes—who needs that on Zoom?). But it could also be because many people started to exercise more during the pandemic as a way to feel purposeful and secure amidst all the horror.

Because the great thing about exercising is that you can do it when, where, and how you want. Your body is with you through it all, no matter what. It is your very own responsibility and can give you direction and purpose when you need it. It rewards you when you take care of it, in the form of increased confidence when you achieve the goals you set for yourself, such as running a little further or lifting a little more. It rubs off on other parts of your life and makes you more daring. And it rewards you with a sense of well-being after exercise that gives you renewed energy to tackle all the other challenges life throws your way.

A study of more than 3,000 Italians found that, on average, they increased their exercise after the coronavirus outbreak. They were also more likely to quit smoking and to eat more healthily. That seemed to be the case for both Americans and Swedes, who, according to the statistics, did increase their purchases of popcorn and chips but, on the other hand, also increased their purchases of fruits and vegetables and healthy drinks such as kombucha.

Eating healthier is just like exercising. In addition to the fact that healthy eating increases the chances of getting those six-pack abs that Adam and God in the Sistine Chapel and the Roman statues have, it also makes your body stronger and healthier and makes it easier for you to live life to the utmost. Like exercise, healthy eating can also provide you with goals and focus when you require them and be a challenge that gives you more confidence to succeed.

There's a whole raft of studies showing how people who feel more purpose in life also eat more healthily, on everyone from American seventh graders and Romanian teenagers, to Portuguese pensioners and Spaniards with eating disorders. But I didn't actually find any on the inverse relationship, whether healthier eating can increase the sense of meaning in one's life. So I went to find out.

In a survey of 500 Swedes, I asked how their lives had changed during the course of the pandemic and found, among other things, that 28% had started to exercise more. I also asked whether they had started to eat more healthily or unhealthily during the pandemic, or whether they had not changed their eating habits at all. Twenty-three percent said they had started eating more unhealthy foods. But almost twice as many, 42%, answered that they had started eating more healthily instead. To see if eating more healthily could increase their perceived sense of meaning in life, I asked half of the people to recall the last time they ate something healthy, while the other half had to remind themselves of the last time they ate something unhealthy, and then asked them if they felt their lives were meaningful. It turned out that those who thought about the last time they ate something healthy rated higher on the scale. Eating healthier thus made them feel that their lives were a little more meaningful.

I repeated the test in a further study (so now there are at least two, to balance the large number of studies testing the inverse relationship...), asking people about the number of times they had eaten healthy versus unhealthy food in the past week and found the same results.

Try eating a little healthier and see for yourself if you notice a difference. Broccoli, for example. It's not very tasty (there are studies on that; almost nobody seems to like the taste the first few times), but it's healthy (that's why there are several studies on what people think of the taste). And precisely because it's not tasty—not in spite of it—it can give you a greater sense of purpose in life. Because you're not eating the broccoli for the short-term reward (which would be a pleasant taste) but because you're making an effort (by eating something that isn't good-tasting) to live a healthier, and thus better, life. You are *templing*. That's solace for when you need it. Actually, we should call healthy eating *comfort eating* from now on and what we used to call comfort eating (ice cream and whatever else) something else. I actually did a study on just that thing—and those who took comfort in ice cream didn't feel much better in the long run...

»WORKING OUT, WHETHER IT'S LIFTING WEIGHTS, RUNNING, BIKING, WALKING WITH POLES, OR DOING WATER AEROBICS, GIVES US A GOAL AND MEANING TO OUR EXISTENCE, RESEARCH SHOWS.«

MORE ROUTINE!

SIGMUND FREUD started every morning by trimming his beard and smoking (as if smoking wasn't dangerous enough without a sharp razor in your other hand).

By contrast, Oprah Winfrey began her day by trimming her body (okay, maybe it was more exercising than trimming, but I hope you'll indulge me in playing with words) first thing through exercise and then trimming her brain with a little Scrabble on her iPad before heading off to the television studio.

Winston Churchill didn't trim at all but stayed in bed for a few hours while he ate breakfast (and yes, while he smoked those big fat cigars, too), read the news and dictated letters to his secretary, before getting up, having a bath and a little walk in the garden and, finally, getting on with the working day (which often began with a three-course lunch).

History doesn't tell us whether spending the morning hour with a razor and cigarette was instrumental in Sigmund forming his pioneering school of psychoanalysis, nor whether the working out and word-pushing made Oprah so successful as the host of the world's most-watched talk show, or whether Winston's morning activities helped him lead Great Britain and the Allies to victory in the Second World War and helped him then win the Nobel Prize for Literature.

But presumably their different, very individual, routines helped to relieve the pressure and stress the three of them were probably feeling, to gather focus and to bring some order to what must often have been very chaotic days. Surely their routines made them perform a little better, just as research shows that athletes' different routines—and they have many, whether it's eating and training the same way every day, calling their mother, wearing the same pair of underwear at a game, reciting the same words, rolling their tongue, slapping their thighs 17 times, or deep breathing—actually make them perform better when it really matters. Maybe their routines also made them feel that their lives had a little bit more meaning.

After all, routines are a way of choosing what it is that we do. Of putting our own stamp on the days of our lives.

As far as I know, no philosopher has ever said that the meaning of life is to have routines (which surprised me a bit, considering how many philosophers there have actually been). But even Aristotle, in his time, thought that we are our actions and coined the word *habitus* to describe both a person's personality and their habits. And while I'm on the subject of vocabulary, I might mention that the word *routine* itself actually means "choice of path" and has its origins in the French word for *road*.

We need routines in our lives. Without them, we risk feeling helplessly suspended in space. Figuratively, of course, but actually also literally. Because it turns out that having a routine is one of the most important factors in ensuring that astronauts maintain their mental function during their long missions in space. In fact, NASA's space mission handbook requires astronauts to create their own routines, which can range from sharing meals to movie times, reading, singing, charades, watching ants, or looking out the window at the same time every day.

The same is true for people in prison. Research shows that routines are a direct predictor of their well-being and their chances of reentering society. The same goes for military personnel. And for people who have been stranded on a desert island (although there are no studies on them as far as I can find—the sample size is probably too small—but in several stories from those who have actually been there and survived), the theme recurs of how they came up with specific things to do every day "just because," like cleaning the beach, counting trees, or pretending to trade coconuts.

Our need for structure is one of the reasons why many people feel a little worse when they lose their jobs or retire, the research shows. I also found research that quantifiably shows that people who feel their time is structured to a greater extent feel that there's more meaning in their lives. After all, jobs (and school) automatically structure much of our time. But having your morning meditation, afternoon walk with the dog, your daily move in an ongoing remote chess match, half-hour reading of a good book in bed at night, or whatever you prefer, are also ways of structuring time.

Moreover, unlike work and school, your routines are a way of structuring your time just the way you want it. Your choice of path, to put it in plain French. They give you a sense of control. Even if you're not the world's most popular talk show host, or leading the free world through a world war, life can feel chaotic and unpredictable. So deciding what to do for a moment in the day, regardless of what else is going on, can be an invaluable way to feel like you actually have some control over your life (and doesn't that make it a little easier to understand why Winston chose to stay in bed for a few hours every morning?).

In a journaling study, people were asked to report how much control they felt they had over their lives each day, and it turned out that on days when they felt more control (for whatever reason), they also felt that their lives were a little more meaningful. For example, having a cup of coffee and looking at people's flower (or maybe moss?) pictures on your favorite accounts for half an hour every afternoon, no matter what's going on, can be a wonderful way to take control of your life.

It can also be a way to practice some mindfulness.

That coffee and flower-watching can work as mindfulness maybe isn't that much of a surprise. But it turns out that doing laundry, the dishes, homework, or just about any routine can actually function as a mindfulness activity. Researchers sent messages to a bunch of American students (who've agreed to that, that is) at random moments six times a day for a week, asking what they were doing.

They were surprisingly quick to respond (perhaps a little too quick in some cases, such as when noting they were "currently watching the second act of a play" or "driving home from a wedding").

The researchers could see a pattern that when students did something that seemed to be a recurring routine during the week, like the examples I just mentioned, students felt they were a little more present (or whatever Swedish synonym you prefer for the English word *mindful*) and at the same time, ticked up slightly higher numbers on the meaning scale.

Routines can be both a way to get going in the morning or before a performance, and a way to stop and just pause. Doing something that shuts out all the noise and uncertainty and focuses your mind on the here and now and being there. It doesn't get much more existential than that, does it?

So my advice to you is to embrace your routines, and maybe even start routinizing (that is, coming up with even more).

Aristotle would probably advise you to see them as expressions of who you are. Personally, I think of them as little breaks that give you time to just be, where and when you are. Little moments when you are in complete control of your life and the universe. That you can look forward to again and again. It doesn't matter what they are, as long as they are your very own, chosen by you. And they don't even have to be really self-chosen. Even doing laundry (which probably often feels more like a chore) can work if you embrace it as a moment to stop and be mindful and make yourself unavailable for a moment for everyone else's (and your own, you stressed-out human!) demands on your time.

Maybe it's even time to come up with some new routines? Let your imagination run wild, find a time in the morning, evening, or any other time of the day or day of the week, and do whatever you feel like (but I suggest that it ideally be something other than trimming your beard and smoking). Here are some routines to get inspired by:

- Author Patricia Highsmith took a moment each day to walk around and collect beautiful snails in her neighborhood. She also had a routine of eating the same food at every meal (though that particular diet, bacon and eggs, might not be recommended).

- Barack Obama didn't eat the same food all the time as part of his routine, but he did wear the same "uniform" every day that he was president (grey suit, white shirt with small stripes and blue tie), which was something he could control no matter what else happened.

- Charles Dickens went for a walk through London every afternoon, Charles Darwin went for a long walk with his dog, while Haruki Murakami instead has a routine of leaving the house at exactly noon every day, wherever he is, to run a mile or swim 1,500 yards.

- Kafka took a three-hour nap every afternoon, a routine also emulated by basketball player LeBron James. Tennis player Serena Williams instead relaxes with an hour of dancing every afternoon.

- Beethoven went to the tavern every night to read the paper. Theodore Roosevelt sat in his car for an hour after driving home and read it before going in the house instead. Susan Sontag took an hour's break every night after dinner to read a good book.

- A Swedish economics professor begins each morning by sending birthday greetings to all his friends whose birthday it is. And eats three Christmas Santa marshmallows every day, all year round.

»WE NEED ROUTINES IN OUR LIVES. WITHOUT THEM WE RISK FEELING AS THOUGH WE'RE HELPLESSLY DRIFTING IN SPACE. METAPHORICALLY OF COURSE, BUT ALSO ACTUALLY LITERALLY. IT TURNS OUT THAT ONE OF THE MOST IMPORTANT FACTORS TO ENSURE THAT ASTRONAUTS MAINTAIN MENTAL FUNCTION DURING THEIR LENGTHY PERIODS IN SPACE IN NAMELY THAT: HAVING ROUTINES.«

MAKE THiNGS UP!

42

IF YOU search on "what is the meaning of life," one of Google's first suggestions is "42." The number appears in Google's search box even before you finish typing the question and hit enter. That's how confident the search engine is that it could be the answer you're looking for, based on the millions of people who have searched or clicked their way to 42 in the past.

Surely you recognize that number (it may even have popped into your head when I asked if you know what the meaning of life is in the introduction to the book). It comes from Douglas Adams' book *The Hitchhiker's Guide to the Galaxy* (which later became a movie of the same name) where, after seven and a half billion years of calculations, the galaxy's biggest supercomputer comes up with the answer to life's biggest question: 42.

Why 42, you might ask (along with all the other people who have searched so diligently that Google suggests you reread it)?

"I just made it up," answered the author Douglas Adams himself, before he died. "As a joke, I wanted a number, something simple. I wrote 42 and that was that."

A simple number can seem like a meaningless answer. But

life is meaningless, according to existential theory. Like death, it is one of the great human questions, one of those that drive us to ponder our existence and seek answers. The idea is echoed by the 19th century philosopher Nietzsche, who, as we have already seen, believed that everything in life was meaningless. His conclusion was that it is therefore up to us to fill existence with some form of meaning. A hundred years later, Jean-Paul Sartre went so far as to say that we are condemned to invent our own meaning because life is disgustingly meaningless, which explains the title of his most famous novel, *Nausea*, which was one of the reasons why the Swedish Academy (after years of hesitation) awarded him the 1964 Nobel Prize in Literature (Sartre was equally hesitant and turned down the prize, but nine years later sent a discreet letter asking if he could still get the money...).

If you click on Google's suggestion, you'll find that people all over the world think the number 42 is a perfectly good answer and have attributed to it all sorts of meanings and significance. For example, that the world's first printed book (which happened to be a Bible) had 42 lines per page, that Elvis died when he was 42, and the speed the *Titanic* was travelling when it hit the iceberg was 42 kilometers per hour. The atomic bomb that destroyed Nagasaki had the explosive power of 42 million sticks of dynamite and a Big Mac contains 42% of the recommended daily intake of salt—the list goes on and on with new connections.

Whether all these people who find new meanings in the number 42 feel greater meaning in their lives has never occurred to any scientist to ask. However, they have asked people who believe in conspiracy theories and similarly look for hidden meanings in things. For example, a Slovakian survey found that people who seek meaning in life are also more likely to look for conspiracies in life. British researchers found a similar correlation when they asked people who had read Dan Brown's book *The Da Vinci Code* (an immensely popular novel, and film, in the early 2000s that launched the idea of a worldwide conspiracy dating back to Leonardo da Vinci) whether they believed in the theory. Those who were searching for meaning in life were more likely to believe it, even when scientists later presented counterevidence to the theory.

There is a whole field of research that shows how we humans like to fill even the most trivial things in life with meaning. It's called teleology and comes from the Greek for "explaining things in terms of their goals."

Aristotle was a big fan of the idea that all things, big and small, have a purpose to achieve. It could be, for example, that the sun radiates heat to give life, that kittens have soft fur to make people want to pet them, or that our hair turns grey as we get older to make us look more distinguished.

None of these explanations are correct, I might add (life, petting, and the sophisticated aura just happen to be nice side effects), because chances are, you intuitively agreed with them. In one of my favorite studies, researchers asked college kids and middle-aged people to rate whether those claims (and a host of others, such as that seawater is made of salt so we won't drink it) are true and found that young people agreed with almost half and middle-aged people with four out of ten. By comparison, they agreed with only 5 and 6% of statements that had no purpose or meaning (for example, that polar bears are white because they swim in cold water, or that thin paper napkins soak up more water).

The researchers also surveyed more than 150 colleagues in the natural and social sciences. Fortunately (I think it's fortunate, of course, as a professor), they were not nearly as likely to agree with the claims of imaginary purposes; only 15% did. But when research colleagues were instead forced to respond under time pressure with no time to think, the figures rose to about a third (oh, well...).

So my advice is to do what Douglas Adams did and make things up. You don't have to make it as hard as trying to figure out the whole meaning of life (people all over the world are still working on grasping the number 42, as evidence shows). It may be enough to find meaning in everyday things—after all, that's what most of life comprises.

For example, in one such study where researchers got unsuspecting people to think about death and thus seek meaning in life, American researchers found that people were more likely to fill everyday activities like brushing their teeth, locking the door, and going to the gym with meaning (such as having a more beautiful smile, making their home safe for their family, and living a healthier life) and to associate them with various goals they had in life. Try being a little teleological yourself when looking at your own Instagram feed. It actually works.

I asked almost 700 people to describe their most recent Instagram post. Half of them only had to describe what was in the picture while the other half also had to be teleological and explain the purpose of the picture. When I then asked how much meaning they felt in their lives, those who had explained the meaning of their latest Instagram picture, whether it was a dinner, a workout, a sunset, a selfie, or something else entirely, on average logged higher numbers on the scale.

Life goes on all the time—pay attention to all the little events and fill them with your own little sentences and life will be more meaningful in the grand scheme of things.

If you're short of ideas, read a book (*The Hitchhiker's Guide to the Galaxy* and *The Da Vinci Code* are two suggestions), or watch a movie. In fact, a Swedish study shows that people find inspiration and ideas for the meaning of life in all sorts of films, from *The Lion King* and *Dirty Dancing* to science fiction movies like *Star Wars* and *The Matrix*.

Speaking of science fiction, every now and then total strangers shout "Cauliflower!" when they see me on the street. I usually have to explain to my puzzled company (if I have some with me at the time) that the person must have seen my show *Chaosology* where I talked about how a person yelling "Cauliflower!" could change the entire universe through a long chain of effects. And that it would actually be enough to just think about shouting "Cauliflower!" to gain power over the rest of your life and the lives of others (by choosing whether to actually shout or stay silent). In the book by the same name I make a longer argument about this and call it *parallel power*, based on theoretical physics about an infinite number of parallel universes (science fiction, like I said ...).

So when I started writing this book, I was curious to learn if those people who have read that book and thought about parallel power might even have a greater sense of purpose in life? I threw the question out on Instagram and got responses from nearly 1,000 book readers; 71% of them said yes.

Whether they really felt that way or just wanted to make me a little happy, I can't know for sure, as this was far from a scientific survey. But just the thought that it might be true gives me a little boost of confidence right now.

And the thought that you might try yelling "Cauliflower!" in some context in the future also makes me happy, so please give it a try. Or come up with something else; it might change the whole universe in the long run and give your life a little more meaning today.

»IN FACT, A SWEDISH STUDY SHOWS THAT PEOPLE FIND INSPIRATION AND IDEAS FOR THE MEANING OF LIFE IN ALL SORTS OF FILMS, FROM THE 'LION KING' AND 'DIRTY DANCING' TO SCIENCE FICTION MOVIES LIKE 'STAR WARS' AND THE 'MATRIX'.«

NARRATIZE YOUR LIFE!

THE WORLD'S FIRST known diary began to be written as early as the 160s, by Marcus Aurelius. The last of Rome's five good emperors, as he was called, wrote down his thoughts on how to deal with his daily challenges and how to ultimately live a good life for himself and for the people of the empire.

The English word for diary actually comes from the Roman Latin *diarium*, which roughly means "daily record." But when the good emperor wrote his diary, that word had not yet been invented. Some say he called it "letters to myself" instead, others say it was called *Meditations*. It's a little unclear and depends on whether you prefer Latin or Greek, which was actually the language Marcus wrote his diary in. He was in fact inspired by the Greek philosophers who were in the habit of justifying their lives in so-called *apologiai*. Aristotle, Socrates, Plato, and Marcus' favorite—Zeno of Cito (the inventor of Stoicism)—the whole gang did it as a training in the art of persuasion and as an opportunity to reflect on how and why they lived their lives.

The Greek philosophers, as we know, preferred to do this

in the form of speech rather than writing. But when the tradition spread to the rest of the world and people began to do it in writing, it became known as autobiography. It's a word we borrowed from the Greek that translates directly to "self narration."

That's also my tip for you. Narratize your life. Create your own autobiography. Write down your life. Talk about it, like the ancient Greeks, or post it on social media if you want to be modern (my guess is that the ancient Greeks would have used YouTube instead if they were alive today).

Anyway, the point is that it worked for these philosophers wise in the ways of life, a Roman emperor, and a whole host of people over the millennia who tried to make sense of their lives by writing in a diary, from the Jewish rebel Josephus in the first century AD and the Christian missionary Augustine in the third century AD to Carl Jung, Franz Kafka, and poor Anne Frank (whose diary we all read in school, didn't we?).

It also jibes quite well with one of the most common definitions of what the meaning of life actually is, namely that meaning is a connection between past, present, and future goals that links events in life (this is why some researchers use so many sub-questions, instead of that single one that I asked you at the beginning of the book).

So it's not particularly surprising that research on people who are nostalgic and enjoy thinking back over their lives shows that, on average, they feel that their lives are more meaningful. Researchers have also asked everyone from college students, to cancer and HIV patients, to 55- to 58-year-old Chicagoans (why they chose people from only that narrow age range isn't clear) to reflect on their lives in the form of life shifts and life stories and found that they had a little boost on the meaning scale in a similar way.

Life narratives are the subject of a field of research unto themselves, showing that we seem to have an innate need to create our own stories in order to understand ourselves and develop. Children start answering questions about what they have done during their days in the form of little stories (which are not always entirely truthful and are therefore called personal fables) as early as the age of three. At puberty, most people develop some form of life story for themselves as a way of making a record of childhood and looking forward to adulthood, which may explain why one study found that the most common age to start writing a diary is 14. Or why German researchers found that the ratio of biographical books young people read (if they read books, that is) at least once a month increases from an average of 14 to 25% from age 12 to age 15.

There are a lot of studies that use diaries to see how different events and experimental actions affect people's perceived meaning in life. Surprisingly, however, I couldn't find a single study that looked at whether diary-writing *in itself* makes people record higher numbers on the scale.

So I did my own study on social media. Strangely, there were no studies on that either, except one that showed that students who are allowed to turn off notifications on their phones and put them out of reach rank slightly higher numbers on the subjective meaningfulness scale a moment later, compared to those who continue to have their phones pinging away within reach. But that study doesn't actually suggest that screens are bad—which is the usual interpretation; you've probably heard about the study in some discussion about reducing screen time—but rather that the slightly more undistracted time and perceived control increases one's feeling of having meaning in their life.

So myself, I compared how often people post on Instagram, Facebook, or blogs, and found that those who post more often actually feel that their lives are a little more meaningful and that the more recently they made a post, the more likely they are to circle a higher number on the scale.

Now you might object that posts on Instagram rarely seem particularly meaningful. But that's the beauty of it; the posts themselves don't have to be permeated with deep thinking about your life. That was hardly what the average diary entry was like back in the day when people wrote diaries, either. Samuel Pepys, who you read about in school—and wondered how that spelling could be pronounced "peeps"—because his world-famous diary was the first to be published for others to read, wrote not only about major events in England, but also about what he ate and wore. The point is that the entries themselves create a continuity and the kind of link between past and present that researchers who focus on the meaning of life talk about.

And I'm pretty sure you'll also see a pattern of meaning in

the feed you create eventually, once you've been creating your life narrative for a while.

It seems to be the case that we humans seem to have an innate ability to seek out and recognize patterns. Babies, for example, look longer at cars with patterns and respond more to sounds that have some kind of pattern. As early as 16 months, children begin to recognize other people's movements and behaviors, but only if they seem deliberate and have some meaning.

Research within the field of meaning processing shows that patterns help us to make sense of life. For example, researchers found that people who were manipulated into feeling out of control (by giving them random feedback that had nothing to do with their performance, or just by asking them to think about situations where they had no control) were more likely to see patterns in the static on televisions screens, in all the dots on a graph of the financial market, or between events like saying the phrase "fingers crossed" at some point and receiving a job offer some time later. In the absence of control, they looked for understandable patterns to impart some kind of meaning. There have also been a number of experiments where people were shown pictures of trees, either in a pattern or out of order (for example, organized by seasonality) or four words that were in a logical order or not, in which researchers found that those people who saw patterns and order experienced both greater meaning in their lives and were more likely to make an effort to undertake different life goals. In one of the most fun experiments, people were allowed to take a one-minute break between writing down their goals and seeing the trees before continuing to fill out a survey on the screen at home. Those who had written down that they wanted to be more fit were more likely to spontaneously do anything during the break, from watching an exercise video on YouTube to lying on the floor and doing push-ups, if they were shown the trees according to seasonality.

So whatever you do throughout the course of your day, and whatever you've been through in your life, I'd recommend you reflect upon it sometimes. See how a pattern emerges in your life, in the small and the big things. How one event follows another. Describe it for yourself, or for someone else, and you'll both feel demonstrably more meaning in your lives. Try to write a diary that people can read 2,000 years from now. Or post photos on Instagram and look at them yourself a little more frequently. It doesn't have to be a lot of words and you don't have to worry about the way you write; the important thing is that you understand it yourself. A few simple words can be enough and no one else needs to see them. And you don't have to be a top-notch photographer or an influencer to take pictures, as long as you yourself know what the pictures represent. You can choose to put them out there for everyone to see, have a private account for just a few other people, or just save them for yourself on your phone.

If you're looking for tips and inspiration, I found in my research that some of the most common posts people recently made on Instagram were:

- Images of scenery, such as a flower, meadow, sunrise, or beautiful place during an evening stroll. Or for that matter, a church or very tall chimney.
- Family, relatives, and friends gathering, doing something together, or celebrating something (even things like annual extended family get-togethers).
- Food that's being prepared, eaten, desired, or grudgingly—but meaningfully—lamented (broccoli!).
- Running, swimming, yoga, and all manner of workouts.
- Entertainment, like a trip to the theater, a game, or a get-away, or hilarious events like body painting, a bad haircut, having an awkward blind date, or accidentally lecturing at the wrong event (guilty!).
- Sad events, like something being lost or stolen, something gone wrong, or someone falling ill.
- Projects, like building a porch, renovating a house, growing nasturtiums under your bed (!), painting, or starting your own business.
- Comments on major events, like an election, a rally, or a tragedy, and participation in movements (#metoo).

- Tips and information for other people, for example about health, where to get things (free electricity in Sundbyberg) or maybe books to read (do you know any good ones about the meaning of life?).

This has to be plenty of material from which you can create exciting, funny, and moving stories?

»RESEARCH ON PEOPLE WHO ARE NOSTALGIC AND ENJOY THINKING BACK OVER THEIR LIVES SHOWS THAT, ON AVERAGE, THEY FEEL THAT THEIR LIVES ARE MORE MEANINGFUL.«

CONNECT!

AT ANFIELD Churchyard in Liverpool, England, which is considered one of the most beautiful in the country (and the world, if you ask the people of Liverpool), a mythical clay bird sits on each and every gravestone.

It's not clear what made it mythical—it has none of the awesome powers of its fictional counterpart, the phoenix, which rises from the ashes—but it's certainly a symbol of Liverpool, whose name in Old English means "mud puddle." The clay bird is also part of the football team's logo, which is on a whole dozen gravestones, I noticed as I walked through the diamond-shaped walkway in the cemetery a few years ago. I know that the people of Liverpool are proud and feel a strong sense of belonging to their mud puddle, but that so many of them wanted to be buried with the football team's club emblem as a memorial surprised me. But since then I have discovered that it's pretty much the same in many other cemeteries and death notices around the world. More and more people seem to be thinking about their favorite teams before their eternal resting place, whether it's Barcelona FC, the LA Lakers or Edsbyn's bandy team (I couldn't find any statistics, but was told by familjesidan.se, which collects all of Sweden's obituaries, that it's now the fourth most common theme, after religious motifs, flowers, and hobby motifs like sailing boats).

There's actually research showing that death makes people more likely to identify with their favorite teams. When researchers asked Dutch students to think about death, they were more likely to cheer for the national football team and expect them to score more goals in the upcoming international match against Germany, as compared to those who were asked to think about a television show. The researchers repeated the experiment on students at the University of Arizona, who also started cheering more for the school's basketball team.

In a way, we humans have a basic need to be part of a team. Existentialist theory contends that the fact that we're born alone (unless we're twins, that is) and that we die alone is one of those ultimate quandaries that make people seek meaning in life. We need to be part of a greater connection for our lives to mean anything. This theme recurs in several religions, from attaining oneness in Buddhism to being part of the chosen people in Judaism, going to heaven in Islam and Christianity, or being at one with nature or the universe in nature religions and New Age practices.

Not surprisingly, there have been several studies on religion in particular, showing that people who believe in God feel a little more as though there's meaning in their lives, whether they are Jewish, Christian, or Muslim (or are Hindu and believe in multiple gods). That nuns and priests rank higher on the meaning-having scale. That people who convert to Christianity or Judaism jump up a bit on the scale (there happened to be surveys on just those two religions, but the same is probably true of other religions, too). And that daily religious activities such as praying or visiting a temple increase the daily perceived nature of the meaning of life.

But context can come in a number of guises. Indeed, it is a recurring theme as researchers interpret and group people's responses to all sorts of things that give meaning to life. When researchers asked American and Indian students to think of occasions that made them feel connected, they circled higher numbers on the meaning scale, no matter what the context was. There have also been experiments in which researchers tricked subjects into thinking they were playing catch with three other people on a screen and when the other people (who were in fact just the computer) threw only to each other, the subjects, who felt disconnected, selected lower numbers on the scale.

In another variation of this study, students are asked to record a short introductory video of themselves in the belief that it will be watched by another person with whom they will collaborate on a group project, and when they are then told that the person has seen the video and declined to work together (scientists can be real sadists...) the poor "rejected" students answered lower on the question of whether they felt their life had meaning.

The need for togetherness and connection may be one of the reasons why many people felt so bad during the global pandemic. Schools and workplaces closed, training sessions were cancelled, people in quarantine weren't allowed to see their families. They are all examples of connections that we humans list highly when asked what gives meaning to our lives, connections that many of us did not think about and took for granted before we were deprived of them. That's why my tip is: connect. Don't wait until your connections disappear before you appreciate them. See them and let them give your life more meaning. Ideally, don't let them vanish at all.

Even if you can't see your family in person—and it doesn't take a pandemic for that to happen with everything else we have going on in life—get in touch with them. Zoom your parents, send them a text message. A simple heart emoji might be enough, if you don't have time to write. Or just think about them; it actually goes a long way for your own sake to remind yourself that they exist and that you're connected.

Myself, I have three stars tattooed on my neck—it was the first tattoo I got—to remind myself every time I look in the mirror of the three stars in my life: my children and their mother. My life is larger than just myself, and it doesn't belong only to me, but to them, too. That tattoo has helped me a lot. I've never really felt part of a greater community, and I've always had a tendency to get lost, both when I'm travelling around the world alone lecturing, and when my thoughts bounce around unrelentingly in my head day and night. The map of stars on my neck reminds me that everything I do somehow affects them and helps me find my way home again.

Family and loved ones, almost always end up at or near the top when people answer what gives meaning to their lives. But family togetherness can also be much bigger than your family members. A study of nearly 600 students at three Los Angeles high schools found that those who identified with, and felt more connection to, others in their ethnic group—no matter how they defined that group—felt greater meaning in their lives (and performed better in school).

The connection can also be the school itself; indeed, in several surveys in which people responded to what gives them meaning in life, they also named their schools. When American researchers followed more than 1,000 teenagers for a year, they could see how school and various school activities steadily contributed to their sense of meaning in life.

The job you go to every day can add meaning to your life, too. Research on everything from American job-seeking students to Swedish schizophrenia patients shows that many associate career choices and work with meaning in their lives—if it's a job that means something to you, that is. Researchers comparing the perceived meaningfulness of jobs among 1,000 people aged 18 to 67 found that the more meaningful people perceived their jobs to be, the less they mulled over the meaning of life... while those who didn't perceive their jobs to be particularly meaningful instead began to reflect more with each passing year. In a survey of 2,000 Britons a few months after the pandemic began, more than 40% said they were considering changing careers to find more meaningful work.

And indeed, your favorite team can also be a connection that provides meaning (even before it's time to write your obituary and choose your headstone). There's research on that, too. American college kids who identify with basketball teams feel greater connection and greater meaning in life, a study shows. Same with New Zealanders who are supporters of their city's rugby team.

You can also form your very own team. It doesn't have to be sports-related; it could just as easily be a Harry Potter club. A survey of the young members of an online community active around the time when the "boy who lived" faced the decisive battle with his archenemy Voldemort in the final film found that the more they identified themselves as Hogwarts fans, the more meaning they felt in life.

Or you can join the retired ladies of the (not unexpectedly) English Sherlock Holmes Society, who gather once a week to solve mysteries. In interviews, they said it gives them both connection and meaning in their lives.

There are so many different connections you can be part of. Take the time to see them and make verbs out of them; turn your point of connection into *a real connection*. Connect with family, friends, school, work, like-minded people and be involved for your own sake and the sake of others. Just thinking the thought more often and feeling it more often can go a long way. It could be a tattoo or a logo. A text message. Or creating a new context. It could be changing jobs or starting your own business. (In a US survey, looking for greater meaning was the most common answer to why people changed jobs. Just under a quarter regretted it afterwards. The others didn't.) Or maybe you can start a club that hunts for moss together?

»WHEN RESEARCHERS ASKED DUTCH STUDENTS TO THINK ABOUT DEATH THEY WERE MORE LIKELY TO CHEER FOR THE NATIONAL SOCCER TEAM, EXPECTING IT TO SCORE MORE GOALS IN THE UPCOMING INTERNATIONAL MATCH AGAINST GERMANY.«

GET BETTER

IN THE MOVIE *Groundhog Day*, cynical TV meteorologist Phil Connors wakes up on a chilly February morning to the sounds of Sonny & Cher's "I Got You Babe" on the clock radio (the film is a few years old...) in a small armpit of a town in the American Midwest, cut off from the outside world by a snowstorm that has interrupted all communication possibilities. Over and over again, he wakes up the same morning to the same song in the same snowy little town.

With no tomorrow and no consequences, Phil begins to live a wildly debauched life, but eventually becomes depressed by the futility and kills himself.

But that doesn't work either; he attempts suicide a whole bunch of times, but comes back to life as soon as the day starts again.

To pass the time, Phil eventually starts taking piano lessons and getting to know the people of the city. It keeps him busy and alive for literally a lifetime. How long the time is supposed to be has been the subject of much discussion over the years; film nerds have looked for clues and time markers and by now have come to a fair agreement that it must be at least 34 years. The screenwriter has said in interviews that it's probably more like 100 years or so, and the director in turn has thrown out 10,000 years. Whatever the case, Phil has time to become both a full-fledged concert pianist and a better man before he finally wakes up to a brand-new morning.

The film has been on the syllabus in introductory philosophy and religion courses at universities around the world, where students discuss everything from Nietzsche's idea of eternal rebirth and Buddhism's doctrine of reincarnation, to what the meaning of life really is. Is it to never give up, to persevere, to get better at piano, or to reach your full potential?

Whether the point is to get better at playing the piano is unclear. But the idea that the meaning of life may be to get better in general seems to be more widely agreed upon. Researchers have found that themes of learning and development recur among teenagers, adults, and retirees around the world when they answer the question. Plato was on the same track in his time, when he put forth the idea that the meaning of life is to attain the highest possible knowledge (whatever that might be. I couldn't find any knowledge about it).

A whole field of research has developed that shows how personal development increases people's perceived meaning in their life and their well-being. Flourishing is what scientists call it.

Like flowers, people need to grow. Those people who seek challenges and strive for personal development feel a greater sense of meaning in life. Studies have been done on both people's professional and personal lives and the results are broadly similar.

In a survey of nearly 14,000 people around the world, researchers found that activities that contribute to personal development were twice as strongly associated with perceived meaning in life as activities that are "merely" pleasurable.

I have found studies that have followed, over time, everyone from Poles to Israeli first-time mothers and grandmothers, Malaysian nurses, and American students who have experienced trauma, all of which show that people who have experienced a sense of themselves as evolving over time feel greater meaning in life. In one experiment, researchers asked one group of people to think about how they had changed over the past year and another group of people to think about how they had stayed the same over that period of time. They found that the first group jumped up a little on the scale of how they experienced meaning in their lives, while the second group instead dropped down a notch.

I have a tattoo on my right forearm of the symbol that appears on signs near road work sites. It is there to remind me that I am not a finished human being, but that my life is a work in progress that will help me improve.

For as long as I can remember, I have struggled with feeling that I'm a bad human being. Whatever I have achieved and accomplished, I have never really gotten rid of the feeling. I still have periods when a kind of hopelessness washes over me and I just want to cease to exist. But the road work symbol helps me to keep going a little bit. The point is that I'm supposed to keep going, I'm not done yet. I'll get better.

But what about improving at the piano?

Yes, even that can give meaning to life. In fact, any instrument seems to work. A study of nearly 200 symphony orchestra musicians found a clear link between how they practiced and felt meaning. And a Korean study of people who had lost their sight found that, like Phil in *Groundhog Day*, they could find meaning in life again by learning to play instruments.

It works with basketball, too. Or water polo. Or dance. There's research on people involved in all three sports that shows how they find meaning by practicing and getting better. Even school works.

A study of over 3,000 Finnish university students showed that those who put in the effort to do better in school felt more purpose in life. And a Korean experiment on 100 college students found that those who received positive feedback on their school performance felt a stronger sense of purpose in life than those who didn't. I even found a study from an American prison that showed how prisoners with life sentences find meaning in their lives by taking courses and improving various skills.

So my advice to you is to get better.

Strive to be and look forward to getting better as a person. Because you will be.

Most people who look back in one, five or 10 years on their lives find that they have changed a lot and that almost all of those changes have made them better (yup, there's a study on that). In other words, you have a lot of growth and flourishing to look forward to in becoming a better version of yourself, even if it doesn't feel that way right now. Dare to believe it; allow yourself to believe it.

And it's actually happening all the time, so keep your eyes open. Researchers contacted 500 people at random times throughout the day over a period of 2 weeks and asked them to describe what they were doing, and how meaningful life felt for them at that moment. They found that people were making small kinds of progress in their jobs or in their private lives and that they actually landed a little higher on the meaningfulness scale during that time. When the researchers asked them if they felt proud, they jumped a little further up on the scale, so let yourself feel pride in your progress.

For help along the way, you can set up small goals. It doesn't need to be a tattoo on your forearm that reminds you that you're a work in progress; it can be that you take on a pound or two more at the gym the next time around. Or even just go to the gym instead of staying home like last time. It turned out to be a pretty common theme when researchers asked a few hundred American students to keep journals about their daily lives for a couple of weeks. Those people who had these kinds of small goals also scored slightly higher on the meaningfulness scale on that same day.

I can't really think of a good way to end this chapter, so I'll just end now. My goal is for the next chapter to have a much better end. I look forward to it. I think the odds of it are pretty good, not least in thinking of what the theme of the next chapter is (read on and find out)...

»JUST LIKE FLOWERS, PEOPLE NEED TO GROW. PEOPLE WHO SEEK OUT CHALLENGES AND STRIVE FOR PERSONAL DEVELOPMENT FEEL A GREATER SENSE OF MEANING IN LIFE. STUDIES HAVE BEEN DONE IN PEOPLE'S PROFESSIONAL AND PRIVATE LIVES AND THE RESULT IS LARGELY THE SAME.«

BE CREATIVE

"**IN MY** art I try to explain life and its meaning to myself," wrote the Norwegian artist Edvard Munch in his diary. Neither the diary nor history tells us whether he succeeded, but he did manage to create the painting *The Scream*.

That's a self-portrait of Edvard standing on a bridge at sunset in the midst of a bout of existential angst. It's also one of the most famous works of art of all time and has spawned the world's most popular Halloween mask (featured in the movies and TV series *Scream*) and that emoji on your phone of a blue-yellow face with its hands at the sides of its mouth that you use when something so horrible happens you don't know what to write.

There are many examples of how art literally means life and death. Among the more ironic is Leonard Warren, who after singing the stanza "to die, a momentous thing" had a heart attack and fell dead on stage at the Metropolitan in New York in the middle of his aria in the opera *The Power of Fate*. Or the world-famous French playwright Molière, who suffered a terrible coughing attack during a performance of the comedy *The Imaginary Invalid* (in which he played the role of the hypochondriac) and had to be carried off the stage (he died a few hours later).

Among the more scientific examples, a study of more than 300 people who had experienced accidents, assaults, terminal illness, and other life-threatening traumas found that they had a greater appreciation of life and were more creative afterwards.

Researchers also subjected students in Boston to a horrific experiment in which they were shown videos of various traumatic events that were randomly selected (including the Holocaust, the 9/11 attacks, and a terminally ill patient). After suffering existential angst, like Edvard Munch, they were given paper and crayons and instructions to draw whatever they wanted. And like Edvard, they felt better when they were done. Which the poor students who were instead instructed to draw geometric figures or solve crosswords did not.

So my advice to you is to create and be creative!

It doesn't have to be to ward off existential angst. Although it seems to work wonderfully in doing just that. There are several examples, such as depressed students who were given a creative writing course having a more positive outlook on life in a follow-up 6 months later, or people who were trained in creative thinking, after being hit hard by Hurricane Katrina in the southern US, having an easier time recovering and finding their way back to life.

But being creative can also bring a greater sense of meaning to life (of course, otherwise there wouldn't be a chapter in this book). In fact, it is listed quite highly in several surveys where people answer what gives them meaning in life.

Younger people in particular rank it highly—among American, Asian, and South African youth alike, it is one of the most common life goals. It doesn't have to be about being a musician, artist, actor, or writer, which young people often associate with their creative life goals. Being creative in any job works great.

An Israeli study of nearly 1,000 people aged 24 to 65 found that the more creative tasks they engaged in and the more effort they put into being creative themselves, the more satisfied they were with their jobs. And the more meaning they felt in their lives, no matter how much they earned, how long their days were, or whether they worked as craftsmen, middle managers, programmers, teachers, or something else entirely.

Work (or school) is a great context in which to be creative, because it is such a big part of every day for many of us. But it works just as well to take it up in your spare time.

British researchers who followed participants in a series of evening courses in singing, writing, and handicrafts found that their average meaning in life score increased over the 7 months the courses lasted.

It doesn't even have to take half an hour, like when you're going to be in nature (in a park or preferably further out into the wild, as you'll remember). At least not if you're writing haiku (which, coincidentally, happen to have nature as their most common theme). When researchers had students write haiku for 20 minutes a day, the students began reporting that they felt greater meaning in life in general after just 3 days.

If you don't feel like taking up poetry, name an elephant instead. At least it worked in one of those studies where people were asked to think about death or the dentist: the former were clearly more creative when they later had to compete to come up with the winning name for the new elephant at the Amsterdam zoo. (Does it work when it's an iguana, too? you might well ask. Well, it did for the scientists, who repeated the test on one, just in case, and got the same result.)

You can also design a T-shirt; for some reason there have been several think-about-death-or-the-dentist-and-and-then-be-creative-active-studies on just that. Or my personal favorite: you can be creatively responsible for organizing a charity event with a (name withheld) rock star. If you get the chance, I really think you should take it. But in the meantime, pretty much anything will do.

When researchers called people at random times of the day (people who had agreed to be called, perhaps I should add. The fact that researchers are happy to subject people to sadistic experiments has been made very clear by now, but calling people without consent is still a step too far...) and asked if they were doing anything creative, one in five people said yes at any given time, reporting that they felt less anxiety and more openness in general about life. In other words, there seem to be plenty of opportunities to be creative at random times of the day if you want to.

However, the researchers did not think to ask this every-fifth-person what they were actually doing creatively at the time. But I did find a meta-study that compiled the creative activities people reported in different contexts, and it showed that they could be anything from music, writing, painting, handicrafts, and various forms of performance to sports, cooking, and (I was thrilled to see) science.

Just pick something, in other words. Do whatever you are divinely inspired to do (yep, there's research on that too, showing that religious people feel closer to God when they are creative).

Be creative and find ways to express your thoughts, feelings, and for that matter your anxieties if you need to, things that you might not otherwise be able to explain to anyone else or to yourself. Be creative by exploring what you can do and what you enjoy doing. Discover that you are not a finished work, one who's done everything already, that it is always possible to create something new in life, to surprise yourself (and probably others too).

It's never too late. An Australian study of 114 women over 80 who took up creative crafts found that they felt a greater sense of purpose in life. So did 36 men and women between the ages of 60 and 93 who entered an art show in Missouri.

But my advice is to not wait. You never know how long you have left. You don't have to stand on a stage in New York singing an aria to face sudden death: a Japanese study that followed 86,000 people over 19 years found that 59 of them died from watching too much television. (Great that you're reading a book instead. Take the opportunity to write a haiku, too, now, while you still can!).

»AN ISRAELI STUDY FOUND THAT THE MORE CREATIVE PURSUITS PEOPLE UNDERTOOK AND THE MORE THEY THEMSELVES MADE AN EFFORT TO BE CREATIVE, THE MORE CONTENT THEY WERE WITH THEIR JOBS, AND THE MORE MEANING THEY FELT IN THEIR LIVES, REGARDLESS OF HOW MUCH THEY EARNED.«

MAKE A DIFFERENCE!

MY GREAT-GRANDFATHER had a huge magnifying glass that I used to play with when I was little; it looked like one of those spatulas they have in the kitchens of hamburger restaurants. He owned it for looking at stamps, but I never saw any except in some old books he had on his overflowing shelf. But he liked to tell me about his own, almost perfect, collection, which he started when my mother was a child and he kept in a safe deposit box. It would be hers, he explained, and it would provide enough for me, too, because it was an almost perfect collection worth a lot of money (and he should know, because he'd written books about that kind of thing himself). He himself lived simply, in the same small, rented apartment, wearing the same worn-out jacket and brown trousers, never indulging in more than a little chocolate every night (a habit my mother, who worked in dentistry, was not entirely fond of, but then again, he had false teeth. Which he should have replaced a long time ago; they chafed him and slipped around), but he was always in a good mood, especially when he went on his weekly visit down to the bank branch.

We never talked about the meaning of life, Great-Grandpa and I; I wish now that we had. But I'm pretty sure that stamp collection made him feel that his life had meaning. I think his working to the last moment to make it perfect is one reason why, despite his frailty (exercising and eating well were never his thing), he lived to be 93, and knowing it would later make a big difference to my mother and me when we sold it meant he didn't need much more in his own life.

I think that stamp collection was his Hoover Dam.

There's a study about it, the big dam out in the middle of the Nevada desert that's become a destination for tourists who need a break from the neon lights and noisy slot machines of Las Vegas.

Researchers have reviewed the many thousands of newspaper articles written about work on the dam that took place in the 1930s and found that when it was criticized for its high costs before and during construction, those responsible almost always argued how much good it would do for posterity in terms of water supply and safety. And hundreds of quotes from those involved at all levels of the construction, from construction workers to truck drivers, cement mixers, canteen staff, and service personnel, testified to the pride they felt afterwards at what they had achieved and the great difference they felt they had made.

Existential theory holds that the last of man's ultimate quandaries is that we are free to do whatever we want. We create our own existence through our actions, and therefore we have the need that what we do should have some meaning. Researchers who measure the meaning of life with long batteries of questions, instead of that one overarching question I asked you, tend to include sub-questions that deal precisely with the feeling of doing something in life that is meaningful and of value.

This may explain why pensioners who are admitted to nursing homes feel less meaning in life as they perceive themselves becoming a burden to their relatives, according to one study. Or why people who lose their jobs and students who stress over not knowing what they want to do after graduation feel similarly less meaningful, according to several other studies. After all, work is such a big part of what we do, or expect to do, for all those hours of the day in our lives.

There is plenty of research on how people who feel they are making a difference in some way at their jobs feel that their lives are more meaningful, whether that's by increasing their employees' well-being or their customers' satisfaction, doing good for society, or the planet and climate, or for that matter by contributing to a company's bottom line. And there's also a bunch of research on how students want meaningful jobs that make a difference to the world and to others in different ways.

In fact, making a difference to the world and doing good for others is one of the most common answers people of all ages give when asked what gives meaning to their lives.

The idea was first put forward by Aristotle, who believed that the meaning of life is to do the highest good, and that's echoed in all the great religions in the form of good lives, good deeds, and good thoughts.

It doesn't have to be a big project like building a dam in the middle of the desert for future generations. It can be giving another person a moment of your time, listening to someone's problems, donating some money, or showing someone appreciation for something they have done—even a simple "thank you" can be enough.

All of these actions are examples of things that increased students' daily sense of meaning in life when researchers asked them to keep diaries of their daily activities over a three-week period. The researchers were also able to establish that they were happy to watch TV, eat snacks, go to parties, drink hard lemonade, and perform a whole host of other activities for their own enjoyment, but without those things making them feel that their life was any more meaningful.

The increase in meaning can also be achieved by getting a stop sign put up at the dangerous intersection in the neighborhood, breaking a new bowling record and getting your name on the wall of the clubroom, or by repainting the entrance to your apartment building.

A study of more than 4,000 Americans between the ages of 24 and 75 found that these were examples of things that made people's lives feel meaningful, along with all sorts of other ways to make an impact.

Just the thought of leaving a mark can be enough to make life more meaningful. People who, at the end of their lives, are able to identify how they have made a lasting difference in some way feel more fulfilled. Treatment trials that allow patients to imagine the mark they could make have helped both heart transplant recipients find their way back to life and drug rehab patients to more easily overcome their addictions.

Perhaps it has to do with biologists' idea that the meaning of life is to reproduce?

If so, that would explain a study that found that people who had sex with their partner felt more meaning in life afterwards. It might also explain why the parents among those 4,000 Americans in the study so often mentioned things that had to do with their children. And also why another study found that people in middle age (which is typically the period when most people reevaluate their life roles) feel a greater need to make imprints in their lives than both younger and older people.

After all, making a mark and passing on your legacy can be done in far more ways than biologically. Like by writing a symphony, for example.

In a rather stunning study, researchers went through all the works of 172 classical composers, from Beethoven and Mozart in the 18th century, Brahms and Tchaikovsky in the 19th century, to Britten and Stravinsky in the 20th century. The study found that the composers seemed (unfortunately, you can't ask them) to exert themselves toward turning their latter symphonies into popular classics. In fact, in general, their last symphonies are shorter, less experimental pieces that are easier to listen to. It seems that all these composers over the centuries have automatically strived to write a final "hit," one that would be played and live on as a legacy long after themselves.

I couldn't find a study on stamp collectors. And there aren't any of them left to ask anymore. Because people may still listen to classical music, but no one is interested in stamps these days.

Several years after my great-grandfather passed away, I went with my mother to the bank vault to pick up his stamp collection. It was indeed almost perfect, as we learned when we put it up for auction. And it certainly would have been worth a lot of money when Great-Grandpa started it. But now the bidding stopped at a few thousand kroner, if that.

I asked my mother when I started writing this chapter, but she didn't remember the amount either, we both just remember how stunned we were, and how we were at first a little sad about Great-Grandpa's inheritance and then burst out laughing in relief when we saw each other's disappointed faces.

Sometimes I wish he'd sold that stamp collection when it had been worth so much and enjoyed the money himself. But then I think of how he always lit up when he told me about it and how Mom and I would get it later. And how that stamp collection in the safe deposit box was probably perfect after all.

»MAKING A DIFFERENCE IN THE WORLD AND DOING GOOD FOR OTHERS IS ACTUALLY ONE OF THE MOST COMMON ANSWERS PEOPLE OF ALL AGES GIVE WHEN ASKED WHAT GIVES MEANING TO LIFE. THE IDEA WAS FIRST PUT FORWARD BY ARISTOTLE, WHO ARGUED THAT THE MEANING OF LIFE IS TO DO THE HIGHEST GOOD, AND IT RECURS IN ALL THE GREAT RELIGIONS IN THE FORM OF GOOD LIVES, DEEDS, AND THOUGHTS.«

LIKE THE SITUATION! (YUP. I'LL SOON EXPLAIN)

THE LIKELIHOOD of picking all the right horses, as Fredrik and his friend had done that day, was almost zero, or more precisely one in just under 36 million. But there on the ticket in his hand he'd marked all the winning horses. It was the only one with all the right ones and the ticket to the entire winning pot of five and a half million kronor, a rather amazingly large sum of money in the late 70s. He hadn't handed it in, because he was a few crowns short of the fee. The friend, who instead handed in his own coupon with a few cancelled horses at half-price, called and cried afterwards. Fredrik himself smiled when he stated in an interview, "We weren't meant to win."

There are quite a few of these kinds of "it wasn't meant to be" quotes online, about races and games that didn't get won, relationships that didn't last, careers that didn't happen, or things that didn't occur (close to a couple of million, I've googled). What the meaning was instead is not clear. But maybe there was some meaning in all those things. In any case, "everything happens for a reason" gives even more Google hits if you search for that phrase. And probably there is a reason for that in and of itself. Like that attitude alone can actually increase a sense of meaning in life, especially when life feels most hopeless—when we don't feel like we're getting better, when we get frustrated at not being able to make a difference, or influence what happens in any way.

Even back in the time of the ancient Greek Zeno of Cito (a favorite of the diary-writing emperor Marcus Aurelius), he was arguing that the meaning of life is, on the whole, to take things in stride, an idea that was developed and carried forward by many famous philosophers of Stoicism. Another word for it is *fortitude*, which is found in many religions. The English word *faith* is even used as a synonym for belief and religion.

The word is confusingly similar to *fate*, which means "destiny." It has a slightly different meaning, but the same approximate conclusion: to be happy with the situation. Likewise with mysticism. The ways of the Lord are inscrutable and all that.

On all those surveys done around the world no one ever seems to have answered that they think the meaning of life is to accept what you have been given. However, it may be part of the reason why many people answer that they feel a sense of purpose in life through religion and spirituality.

In any case, my advice is to accept the situation when you can't influence it. In Swedish, we say *gilla läget*, which translates to something along the lines of "like the situation." Of course, you don't have to like it (but why not—if even gloomy Swedes are willing to give it a go, there might be something to it?); the point is to not regret and be frustrated over something you have no control over anyway. Because our need for meaning is so strong that it can feel quite terrible when we don't find or manage to create it ourselves.

A study of a few hundred unemployed Germans found that feelings of powerlessness and meaninglessness were the main reasons why many felt bad, unable to influence or make sense of why they lost their jobs or didn't get the ones they were looking for.

The same was found by researchers who followed Canadian women who had rheumatism or fibromyalgia over a 10-year period, as well as Nigerian researchers who interviewed students with suicidal thoughts, and researchers who studied both depressed pensioners and addicted youth in California.

Of course, "liking the situation" isn't easy; it's much easier said than done. I myself struggled with my messed-up ears throughout my childhood. From the time I was six, when they were singled out as the reason why I had the TV on full blast, I was in and out of the hospital for operations all the way through my teens.

It was hard and I was embarrassed. I grew long hair to hide the scars and the tape my mother put over my ears so they wouldn't stick out, and I went to a speech therapist to learn how to speak cleanly because I couldn't hear how to sound "right."

Why my ears wouldn't work we never really got right.

Maybe it would have been solved eventually if I had kept going in for surgery (and I'm very grateful to my fantastic doctor who never stopped trying), but when I decided that my ears and hearing had to be the way they are, I finally started to feel better. "There's probably a reason for that," I remember my mother saying, and many years later I tattooed a "mute the sound" symbol on my hand as a reminder.

It turns out it's a bit the same with people who suffer from tinnitus, according to an American study of 300 patients. Those who struggled with the futility of their condition and couldn't stop asking themselves why they were suffering felt less meaning in life than those who decided that it was just going to be that way.

And there is research on people who have experienced far more serious things than ringing in the ears. An English doctoral thesis followed parents of children with serious illnesses and injuries and found the same pattern in how, after much frustration and despair, they landed on the fact that there must be some meaning to it all, even if they didn't yet know what that meaning was.

There have also been treatment studies on both Indian and Norwegian cancer patients, people who have lost a life partner, and people with severe death anxiety who, by gradually accepting their situations, were able to find their way back to some form of enthusiasm for life.

We humans like to find reasons for everything. Children are prone to making up almost anything to explain why things are the way they are, studies show. And as I mentioned in the chapter on "making things up," without time to think about it, even scientists think it makes sense that the sun shines to provide warmth and that people get grey hair so that they will look distinguished.

That's why it's particularly difficult and meaningless when we fail to find the reason or create meaning when we need it most. And that's why it becomes extra important to allow ourselves to accept what's happening and what is, without having to understand.

Although there is probably hardly a single person who has never heard (and probably everyone has at some point used) the expression "everything happens for a reason," I did not find any study that found out how many people actually believe it to be true. I got curious and threw out the question on my Instagram, "Does everything happen for a reason?" Within 24 hours, I had received close to 2,000 responses, divided into two fairly even halves: 55% believed it was true that everything happens for a reason; 45% didn't believe it.

That made me even more curious; does it matter which half you belong to? I asked 500 people if they agreed with the statement and then asked them to circle a number on the meaning scale, and it turned out that those who believed that everything happens for a reason felt a little more meaning in life than the others.

Whether it's actually true that everything happens for a reason, we'll probably never know (but if it is true, then there's a reason we won't know, and that in itself is a pretty comforting thought, I think). But at least now we know that it is possible to feel a little more meaning in life by being content to believe that it is there, in both the big and the small things.

Personally, I think of it as a way of not taking things too seriously. That can save me unnecessary grief over not being able to influence them anyway (like the price of a near-perfect stamp collection when someone put it up for auction way too late) and as a lifeline when I need meaning the most and all those other tips aren't working. It may sound glib to like the situation (and in a way it is), but to do so, to accept things and have faith, may also be the most profound meaning of all.

»AN ENGLISH DISSERTATION FOLLOWED PARENTS OF CHILDREN WITH SERIOUS ILLNESSES AND INJURIES AND FOUND THE SAME PATTERN IN THE WAY, AFTER MUCH FRUSTRATION AND CONFUSION, THEY ARRIVED AT THE THOUGHT THAT THERE MUST BE SOME MEANING TO IT ALL, EVEN IF THEY DIDN'T YET KNOW WHAT THAT MEANING WAS.«

SEARCH (AND BE OPEN TO WHAT YOU FIND)

THE DESERT IN Black Rock, Nevada is scorching hot during the day and the ground is, as the name suggests, rock-hard, as anyone who's been there knows. But that didn't deter one farmer in 1916 who decided to start a farm there. Since no one else even thought of moving out into the desert, the price of land was very cheap. All that was needed was a well, reasoned the farmer, who used the money he had left over to buy digging equipment. If he looked hard enough, he would probably find both a way to break through the rock-hard ground and a place where there was water.

No one seems to know exactly how long he searched, but in his last attempt he did indeed find water. But not the cold water he had wanted for a well—boiling water.

There was no well and no farming for the farmer. But when a heating company returned to the abandoned farmhouse to dig 50 years later, they discovered that the boiling water had created a beautiful little geyser in the middle of the desert. Today, people from all over the world flock to the Fly Geyser, and it has become part of the mythical Burning Man festival where people go to explore themselves and each other.

So the farmer didn't find what he was looking for and was probably frustrated, to say the least. In the same way, Viktor Frankl, when he introduced the idea of man's need for meaning in life, argued that the search for it makes it more difficult to find, and increases the frustration of not having it already.

At this point in time, there have also been a number of studies showing that people who search for meaning experience less of it and range from being more stressed, neurotic, and insecure, to less happy.

The situation is particularly bad in middle age, several studies show. The fact that middle age in one of these studies was given as the range from 26 (!) to 44 is enough to make one stressed and neurotic in itself. The only study I can find that shows the opposite, that those who search for meaning in life also experience more of it and feel better, is a study of 1,000 Japanese people.

So my advice would be not to search for meaning in life if you are not Japanese.

Or to think like the Japanese and search for meaning in life.

The researchers who did the study on the Japanese thought that the explanation for why they felt more meaning when they searched for it, rather than less (as was the case with the 1,000 Americans the researchers compared them to in the same study), is that the Japanese don't think of a happily-ever-after in which there's some finish line to aim for. Instead, they are more open to what could pop up along the way anywhere, and at any time.

In other words, it can actually be good to search for meaning in life as long as you don't aim too narrowly. Be open to what you might find, which was my point with the farmer in Black Rock.

Like the Americans in that study, he got frustrated (we can assume, since no one asked him) and moved off the farm when he didn't find what he was looking for. But if he had been Japanese instead (or at least thought like one), he might have seen the amazing geyser he missed because he was all about his cold-water well.

There are many examples of people who searched for something but in the end found something more important than what they were looking for. Christopher Columbus was looking for a quicker route to India but "discovered" America instead (though he himself insisted that it was actually India).

An opal digger in Australia found a previously unknown species of dinosaur recently instead of the gems he was after. Some kids digging for worms in Jämtland found a Viking treasure, and police in Norrköping who went to help a man look for his missing hunting rifles instead found a cannabis stash that his 64-year-old roommate had hidden under his bed. Of course, this didn't make the man with the rifles any happier (and certainly not his partner), but the cops were delighted.

What if it's the same with searching for meaning in life? That it can lead you to find other things that are important in life if you're open to it?

Researchers who followed more than 400 Romanian secondary school students found that those who were more likely to search for meaning in life had, on average, started exercising more, ate better, and were doing better in school a year later. The same was true for about 100 people who tried to quit smoking; those who sought meaning were more successful. And a study of people who survived the 2013 Colorado flood disaster found that those who were searching for meaning in life were more likely than others to feel they had developed as people a year later. Unfortunately, the researchers in these cases didn't think to also ask the people if they also felt that their lives a year later were more meaningful (perhaps the researchers thought that was pointless).

»RESEARCHERS CONTEND THAT JAPANESE PEOPLE DON'T THINK ABOUT A HAPPILY-EVER-AFTER WHERE THERE'S A FINISH LINE TO AIM FOR. INSTEAD, BE MORE OPEN TO WHAT COULD POP UP ALONG THE WAY— WHENEVER AND WHEREVER.«

DON'T
GIVE UP

THE BLOOD CANCER didn't take my father. I barely saw him for the next year after that phone call; he went through several tough rounds of chemo treatments and couldn't manage to do more than send a text message once in a while. And then it was to let me know that at least he was alive. But amazingly, new treatments were developed during that year, which he was able to try the following year. They both kept the cancer in his blood at bay and allowed him to retain a little more energy. We were able to see each other for short periods of time and he was able to go on outings away from home and the hospital. But pretty soon he started to be unsteady when he walked, and when he finally fell over one day, they x-rayed his brain and found a tumor so big that there was no point in even trying to take it out.

Instead, he was put on a program where they tried to blast the tumor from different angles. I remember how they drilled holes into his skull and screwed a big tripod around his head. There were quite a few test shots, and in the meantime his memory, speech, and body control all deteriorated (he looked, walked, and sounded a bit like Frankenstein's monster, now that I think about it).

Despite all the trials and radiation, which Dad described as making his brain feel like an egg in boiling water, the tumor could not be made to disappear. But it did eventually shrink to the point where it was no longer life-threatening. And after years of treatments, tests one day showed that the incurable cancer in his blood was actually...cured.

More than 10 years after our lunch and that phone call, my dad is still alive. Cured of the blood cancer and with a radiated tumor in his head that has impacted most of his daily life and left him unable to read (something he truly loved) but is held in check. But some time ago he woke up with terrible stomach pains which turned out to be a large tumor in his stomach and now he is back on a new chemo program.

When I started writing this book, I asked to talk to him about how he saw the meaning of life, what he was thinking when he got that first devastating diagnosis, and how he got through all those years of tough treatments. We had to postpone the conversation a few times because he was too unwell, but once we sat down together, we talked in a way we had did in my life.

He told me how he thought about his wife, me, and my children when he got the news. How he didn't want to leave her alone, how he wanted to be sure we would all make it through. He said he still felt too curious about what the future holds for us ("The kids have their whole lives ahead of them and with you, you never know."). We talked about how we both have that general irrepressible curiosity in common, how I can't help but explore everything, and we talked about all things medical and technological, including human advances that will be made in the future. He told me how, in the midst of all his trouble, after the first announcement and before each new treatment, he was also actually a little curious about how it was going to play out, what was going to happen, and how it was going to work.

I found a study about this (I was, of course, curious and looking). It showed that people who are curious feel a bit more of a sense of meaning in life, and that the curiosity people report in their diary that they feel on a given day also increases their perceived meaning of life on that particular day.

I asked him about the moments when it was at its worst. When he was screwed to an iron tripod and couldn't talk or move. When the chemo made him feel so bad that he couldn't think a single thought or get out of bed. When he was told for the third time that he was probably screwed.

What did he think?

He pondered, wrestling with his words. "It'll all work out," he said in the end.

We talked about how he's not religious—far from it—but how he's always believed that somehow life is meant to be solved. And the religious connections are hard not to make, to the trials of the Lord and the saying that God does not give you greater burdens than you can bear. To the karma of Buddhism and Hinduism.

"It has to all work out," he concluded.

For some reason I remembered when I was 12 years old

and staying over with him and his wife on weekends. We were playing video games and with the quick reflexes of a 12-year-old I had no problem steering the spaceship through all the obstacles and surviving, while Dad had to struggle to get even halfway. At night when I got up to pee, I could see him in the light from the TV screen as he sat in the dark, trying over and over and over again.

That happened more than one night and by the end I remember him digging out his winter gloves in the middle of summer to hold the controller because of the chafing he got on his sweaty hands. Maybe it's a weird connection. I'm not sure why it came to mind.

But maybe all of life is, in fact, a video game. Techno-philosophers and theoretical physicists sometimes talk about the simulation hypothesis—half in jest and half in earnest—which contends that we humans might just be simulated characters in some more advanced creature or machine's game console.

But even if life isn't a video game, maybe it is like a video game? Which is about surviving as long as possible, as Darwin and the biologists believed. Perhaps life itself is the duty Kant talked about, the one we must never give up?

A large study of almost 8,000 people in 109 countries found a positive correlation between the propensity to struggle through life no matter what (English has a word for it, grit, which we lack in Swedish) and well-being and meaningfulness.

In another study, the same propensity to never give up was shown to increase students' perceived meaning in life and reduce the number of depressive thoughts in the following month.

Dad told us how he was not expecting any of the cancer diagnoses, yet somehow he was not surprised. Life is constantly coming up with new things to cope with. Sooner or later, the degree of difficulty increases again.

We talked about how it's possible to think of it a bit like levels or reincarnations, on the way to salvation or nirvana. But Dad preferred the analogy of the levels in a video game, where each level has new challenges.

I was looking for a study on that, too. The closest I found was one in which students who listed a number of factors in their education, such as workload and learning difficulties, as challenges rather than obstacles felt better and got more out of life in the following 10 weeks.

For as long as I can remember, my dad has always Loved (no lower case "l" here) meat and sausages: in restaurants, frying at home, and most of all barbecues. That's why I was pretty surprised when he told me that he was going to eat vegetables for dinner when we finished our conversation. Just vegetables. No more meat or sausages, to improve his chances of fighting stomach cancer. No thought that it wouldn't matter so much at this point, in treatment or life, or that he'd rather treat himself to something in the midst of all the hardship.

"Gloves on?" I suggested.

"Gloves on," he replied.

I think of that car again, driving around shouting "Think about death!" from the loudspeaker on the roof. Maybe a reminder of death makes us feel that life has more meaning because it reminds us that life is worth fighting for and that we are now on the last old man (of those three that usually appear in the video games to represent how many lives the player has left) and that now is the time to fight like never before.

So my last tip to you is to put on your gloves and eat vegetables (preferably broccoli, if you don't like it). Or do whatever you can to increase your chances of survival. No matter how difficult and hard it feels.

See the obstacles in your way as challenges. Don't give up. Be curious about what happens when you take them on and refuse to give up. Remind yourself when life is hard that it doesn't have to mean you're doing something wrong—you're actually doing something right. You may have reached a new level of difficulty and if you don't give up, life will eventually reach another level of difficulty.

Life is for hanging on, pushing through, leveling up, not for giving up on. Life is too amazing to give up.

»BUT EVEN IF LIFE ISN'T A VIDEO GAME, MAYBE IT'S LIKE A VIDEO GAME? FOR WHICH THE POINT IS TO LIVE AS LONG AS POSSIBLE, LIKE DARWIN AND THE OTHER BIOLOGISTS CONTENDED. MAYBE LIFE ITSELF IS THE DUTY THAT KANT SPOKE ABOUT, THE ONE WHICH WE CAN NEVER GIVE UP?«

BY THE WAY

BUT WHAT was that about riding a motorcycle? You might be wondering by this point. (And if you're not it's more than time that you start cultivating a little more curiosity; it increases your sense of meaning in your life, you know that, right?)

Well, I did promise to come back to it when, in the chapter about "templing," I described how riding a motorcycle found itself at the top of the list on what the meaning of life was in the Swedish Church's web survey from 2007.

Here's the way it happened. Anyone who wanted to could take part in the Swedish Church's survey, and in the end it became the largest in the world with over 30,000 participants. Anyone who wanted to could also offer their own suggestions about the meaning of life, that other people could vote on.

Some of the suggestions that came in were to find Jesus, Bajen (a popular Swedish soccer team), brass bands—and of course the number 42. But none of these suggestions ranked very high in the vote tally. Instead, the top 10 suggestions comprised nine anticipated recommendations (at least for those of you who have read this book), like doing good deeds, being healthy, feeling good, and being needed, and in first place, with 8% of all votes, the significantly more unexpected suggestion about motorcycle riding.

I contacted the press office of the Church of Sweden and asked what they thought was the reason that almost two and a half thousand people cast their votes that the meaning of life is to ride a motorcycle, but there was no one still there who could actually remember how the survey had been conducted. I also contacted the Swedish Motorcyclists Association who replied that they were not surprised, but they had no explanation (maybe they just thought it was self-evident).

This is how I think it happened. The proposals that quickly got a lot of votes appeared at the top of the rankings of the almost 400 that came in, and since no one has the patience to scroll very far down a list, people kept voting for the top proposals.

So Jesus, the brass band, or even the number 42 didn't stand a chance against the more spine-tinglingly plausible suggestions like feeling good and being needed. Probably almost no one even saw them.

But for some reason, "riding a motorcycle" fast ended up being high on the list, perhaps because it simply happened to be one of the first suggestions someone wrote (or because whoever wrote it wanted to create their own little "Hoover Dam" and told all their friends to go in and vote). And when the proposal was up there for all to see, it stood out as a pretty amusing option from among the others, which many people chose for fun.

Or maybe it's true that the meaning of life is to ride a motorcycle? Just to be sure, I asked 1,000 Swedes what they thought gave most meaning to their lives.

No one wrote riding a motorcycle. On the other hand, all the other tips mentioned in this book were mentioned, but also quirkier things like golf, "my guitar," "my cat," "a better ass," and "three of my children" (which makes you wonder how many children the person has and what the other children have done to their poor parents...). There were so many of the quirkier suggestions that I could write a new little book about The Quirky Meaning of Life at some point (so, are you curious now?)

SOURCES

WHAT'S THE POINT?

Fahlman, S. A., Mercer, K. B., Gaskovski, P., Eastwood, A. E. & Eastwood, J. D. (2009). Does a lack of life meaning cause boredom? Results from psychometric, longitudinal, and experimental analyses. *Journal of Social and Clinical Psychology*, *28*(3), 307–340.

King, L. A., Hicks, J. A., Krull, J. L. & Del Gaiso, A. K. (2006). Positive affect and the experience of meaning in life. *Journal of Personality and Social Psychology*, *90*(1), 179–196.

Ryff, C. D. & Dunn, D. D. (1985). A life-span developmental approach to the study of stressful events. *Journal of Applied Developmental Psychology*, *6*(2–3), 113–127.

Steger, M. F. (2012). Experiencing meaning in life: Optimal functioning at the nexus of well-being, psychopathology, and spirituality. I: P. T. P. Wong (red.), *Personality and clinical psychology series. The human quest for meaning: Theories, research, and applications* (165–184). Routledge/ Taylor & Francis Group.

Steger, M. F., Frazier, P., Oishi, S. & Kaler, M. (2006). The meaning in life questionnaire: Assessing the presence of and search for meaning in life. *Journal of Counseling Psychology*, *53*(1), 80–93.

Steger, M. F., Mann, J. R., Michels, P. & Cooper, T. C. (2009). Meaning in life, anxiety, depression, and general health among smoking cessation patients. *Journal of Psychosomatic Research*, *67*(4), 353–358.

Zheng, X. & Wang, W. (2020). Whose time flies: Meaning in life influences time awareness. *Journal of Adult Development*, 1–9.

Zika, S. & Chamberlain, K. (1992). On the relation between meaning in life and psychological well-being. *British Journal of Psychology*, *83*(1), 133–145.

THINK ABOUT DEATH

Ai, A. L., Cascio, T., Santangelo, L. K. & Evans-Campbell, T. (2005). Hope, meaning, and growth following the September 11, 2001, terrorist attacks. *Journal of Interpersonal Violence*, 20, 523–548 Fung.

H. H. & Carstensen, L. L. (2006). Goals change when life's fragility is primed: Lessons learned from older adults, the September 11 attacks and sars. *Social Cognition*, 24(3), 248–278.

Boyraz, G., Horne, S. G. & Sayger, T. V. (2012). Finding meaning in loss: The mediating role of social support between personality and two construals of meaning. *Death Studies*, 36(6), 519–540.

Cozzolino, P. J. & Blackie, L. E. (2013). I die, therefore I am: The pursuit of meaning in the light of death. I: J. A. Hicks &

C. Routledge (Ed.), *The experience of meaning in life. Classical perspectives, emerging themes, and controversies* (s. 31–45). Springer, Dordrecht.

Cozzolino, P. J., Sheldon, K. M., Schachtman, T. R. & Meyers, L. S. (2009). Limited time perspective, values, and greed: Imagining a limited future reduces avarice in extrinsic people. *Journal of Research in Personality*, 43(3), 399–408.

Cozzolino, P. J., Staples, A. D., Meyers, L. S. & Samboceti, J. (2004). Greed, death, and values: From terror management to transcendence management theory. *Personality and Social Psychology Bulletin*, 30(3), 278–292.

Cozzolino, P. J. (2006). Death contemplation, growth, and defense: Converging evidence of dual-existential systems? *Psychological Inquiry*, 17(4), 278–287.

Davis, C. G. & McKearney, J. M. (2003). How do people grow from their experience with trauma or loss? *Journal of Social and Clinical Psychology*, 22(5), 477–492.

Davis, C. G., Nolen-Hoeksema, S. & Larson, J. (1998). Making sense of loss and benefiting from the experience: two construals of meaning. *Journal of Personality and Social Psychology*, 75(2), 561–574.

Florian, V. & Mikulincer, M. (1997). Fear of death and the judgment of social transgressions: A multidimensional test of terror management theory. *Journal of Personality and Social Psychology*, 73(2), 369–380.

Florian, V. & Mikulincer, M. (1998). Terror management in childhood: Does death conceptualization moderate the effects of mortality salience on acceptance of similar and different others? *Personality and Social Psychology Bulletin*, 24, 1104–1112.

Hicks, J. A. & Routledge, C. (2013). *The experience of meaning in life. Classical perspectives, emerging themes, and controversies.* Dordrecht: Springer.

Kosloff, S. & Greenberg, J. (2009). Pearls in the desert: Death reminders provoke immediate derogation of extrinsic goals, but delayed inflation. *Journal of Experimental Social Psychology*, 45(1), 197–203.

Landau, M. J., Greenberg, J., Solomon, S., Pyszczynski, T. & Martens, A. (2006). Windows into nothingness: Terror management, meaninglessness, and negative reactions to modern art. *Journal of Personality and Social Psychology*, 90(6), 879–892.

Maxfield, M., Pyszczynski, T., Kluck, B., Cox, C. R., Greenberg, J., Solomon, S. & Weise, D. (2007). Age-related differences in responses to thoughts of one's own death: Mortality salience and judgments of moral transgressions. *Psychology and Aging*, 22(2), 341–353.

Ma-Kellams, C. & Blascovich, J. (2012). Enjoying life in the face of death: East–West differences in responses to mortality salience. *Journal of Personality and Social Psychology*, 103(5), 773–786.

Pyszczynski, T., Wicklund, R. A., Floresky, S., Gauch, G., Koch, S., Solomon, S. & Greenberg, J. (1996). Whistling in the dark: Exaggerated estimates of social consensus in response to incidental reminders of mortality. *Psychological Science*, 7, 332–336.

Routledge, C., Arndt, J., Sedikides, C. & Wildschut, T. (2008). A blast from the past: The terror management function of nostalgia. *Journal of Experimental Social Psychology*, 44(1), 132–140.

Rosenblatt, A., Greenberg, J., Solomon, S., Pyszczynski, T. & Lyon, D. (1989). Evidence for terror management theory: I. The effects of mortality salience on reactions to those who violate or uphold cultural values. *Journal of Personality and Social Psychology*, 57(4), 681–690.

Schwaninger, J., Eisenberg, P. R., Schechtman, K. B. & Weiss, A. N. (2002). A prospective analysis of near-death experiences in cardiac arrest patients. *Journal of Near-Death Studies*, 20(4), 215–232.

Simon, L., Arndt, J., Greenberg, J., Pyszczynski, T. & Solomon, S. (1998). Terror management and meaning: Evidence that the opportunity to defend the worldview in response to mortality salience increases the meaningfulness of life in the mildly depressed. *Journal of Personality*, *66*(3), 359–382.

Steger, M. F., Frazier, P. & Zacchanini, J. L. (2008). Terrorism in two cultures: Traumatization and existential protective factors following the September 11th attacks and the Madrid train bombings. *Journal of Trauma and Loss*, *13*(6), 511–527.

Taubman-Ben-Ari, O. (2011). Is the meaning of life also the meaning of death? A terror management perspective reply. *Journal of Happiness Studies*, *12*(3), 385–399.

Trzebiński, J., Cabański, M. & Czarnecka, J. Z. (2020). Reaction to the COVID-19 pandemic: the influence of meaning in life, life satisfaction, and assumptions on world orderliness and positivity. *Journal of Loss and Trauma*, *25*(6–7), 544–557.

Vail III, K. E., Juhl, J., Arndt, J., Vess, M., Routledge, C. & Rutjens, B. T. (2012). When death is good for life: Considering the positive trajectories of terror management. *Personality and Social Psychology Review*, *16*(4), 303–329.

Wilde, D. J. & Murray, C. D. (2009). The evolving self: finding meaning in near-death experiences using Interpretative Phenomenological Analysis. *Mental Health, Religion and Culture*, *12*(3), 223–239.

NATUREWATCH!

Berman, M. G., Jonides, J. & Kaplan, S. (2008). The cognitive benefits of interacting with nature. *Psychological Science*, *19*(12), 1207–1212.

Berman, M. G., Kross, E., Krpan, K. M., Askren, M. K., Burson, A., Deldin, P. J., ... & Jonides, J. (2012). Interacting with nature improves cognition and affect for individuals with depression. *Journal of Affective Disorders*, *140*(3), 300–305.

Buchanan, E. M. (2019). Modeling resilience, meaning in life, posttraumatic growth, and disaster preparedness with two samples of tornado survivors. *Traumatology*, *26*(3), 266–277.
Cervinka, R., Röderer, K. & Hefler, E. (2012). Are nature lovers happy? On various indicators of well-being and connectedness with nature. *Journal of Health Psychology*, *17*(3), 379–388.
Drescher, C. F., Baczwaski, B. J., Walters, A. B., Aiena, B. J., Schulenberg, S. E. & Johnson, L. R. (2012). Coping with an ecological disaster: The role of perceived meaning in life and self- efficacy following the Gulf oil spill. *Ecopsychology*, 4(1), 56–63.
Fegg, M. J., Kramer, M., Bausewein, C. & Borasio, G. D. (2007). Meaning in life in the Federal Republic of Germany: results of a representative survey with the Schedule for Meaning in Life Evaluation (SMiLE). *Health and Quality of Life Outcomes*, *5*(1), 59.
Flitcroft, D. I. (2012). The complex interactions of retinal, optical and environmental factors in myopia aetiology. *Progress in retinal and eye research*, 31(6), 622–660.
Frumkin, H. (2001). Beyond toxicity: human health and the natural environment. *American Journal of Preventive Medicine*, 20(3), 234– 240.
Hamann, G. A. & Ivtzan, I. (2016). 30 minutes in nature a day can increase mood, well-being, meaning in life and mindfulness: effects of a pilot programme. *Social Inquiry into Well-Being*, 2(2), 34–46.
Howell, A. J., Passmore, H. A. & Buro, K. (2013). Meaning in nature: Meaning in life as a mediator of the relationship between nature connectedness and well-being. *Journal of Happiness Studies*, 14(6), 1681–1696.
O'Connor, K. & Chamberlain, K. (1996). Dimensions of life meaning: A qualitative investigation at mid-life. *British Journal of Psychology*, 87(3), 461–477.
Ojala, M. (2012). How do children cope with global climate change? Coping strategies, engagement, and well-being. *Journal of Environmental Psychology*, 32(3), 225–233.
Ojala, M. (2013). Coping with climate change among adolescents: Implications for subjective well-being and environmental engagement. *Sustainability*, *5*(5), 2191–2209.

Pew Research Center. (2018, 20 November). Where Americans find meaning in life. Accessed on 2020-10-23 from: https://www.pewforum.org/2018/11/20/where-americans-find-meaning-in-life/

Priest, P. (2007). The healing balm effect: Using a walking group to feel better. *Journal of Health Psychology*, *12*(1), 36–52.

Ryan, R. M., Weinstein, N., Bernstein, J., Brown, K. W., Mistretta, L. & Gagne, M. (2010). Vitalizing effects of being outdoors and in nature. *Journal of Environmental Psychology*, *30*(2), 159–168.

Steger, M. F., Shim, Y., Rush, B. R., Brueske, L. A., Shin, J. Y. & Merriman, L. A. (2013). The mind's eye: A photographic method for understanding meaning in people's lives. *The Journal of Positive Psychology*, *8*(6), 530–542.

Steger, M. F., Shim, Y., Barenz, J. & Shin, J. Y. (2014). Through the windows of the soul: A pilot study using photography to enhance meaning in life. *Journal of Contextual Behavioral Science*, 3(1), 27–30.

Weber, M. C., Pavlacic, J. M., Gawlik, E. A., Schulenberg, S. E. &

Zhang, Z. (2019). Outdoor group activity, depression, and subjective well-being among retirees of China: the mediating role of meaning in life. *Journal of Health Psychology*, *24*(9), 1245–1256.

TEMPLE! (A VERB)

Burke, S. M., Brunet, J., Sabiston, C. M., Jack, S., Grocott, M. P. & West, M. A. (2013). Patients' perceptions of quality of life during active treatment for locally advanced rectal cancer: the importance of preoperative exercise. *Supportive Care in Cancer*, *21*(12), 3345–3353.

Choi, Y. H. & Kim, N. Y. (2013). The effects of an exercise program using a resident volunteer as a lay health leader for elders' physical fitness, cognitive function, depression, and quality of life. *Journal of Korean Academy of Community Health Nursing*, 24(3), 346–357.

Conner, T. S., Brookie, K. L., Richardson, A. C. & Polak, M. A. (2015). On carrots and curiosity: eating fruit and vegetables is associated with greater flourishing in daily life. *British Journal of Health Psychology*, 20(2), 413–427.

Di Renzo, L., Gualtieri, P., Pivari, F., Soldati, L., Attinà, A., Cinelli, G. ... & Esposito, E. (2020). Eating habits and lifestyle changes during COVID-19 lockdown: an Italian survey. *Journal of Translational Medicine*, *18*(1), 1–15.

Edwards, S. (2006). Physical exercise and psychological well- being. *South African Journal of Psychology*, *36*(2), 357–373.

Eriksson, B. M., Arne, M. & Ahlgren, C. (2013). Keep moving to retain the healthy self: the meaning of physical exercise in individuals with Parkinson's disease. *Disability and Rehabilitation*, *35*(26), 2237–2244.

Kashdan, T. B., Goodman, F. R., Stiksma, M., Milius, C. R. & McKnight, P. E. (2018). Sexuality leads to boosts in mood and meaning in life with no evidence for the reverse direction: A daily diary investigation. *Emotion*, *18*(4), 563–576.

Lundkvist, P., Fjellström, C., Sidenvall, B., Lumbers, M. & Raats, M. (2010). Management of healthy eating in everyday life among senior Europeans. *Appetite*, *55*(3), 616–622.

Lytle, L. A., Varnell, S., Murray, D. M., Story, M., Perry, C., Birnbaum, A. S. & Kubik, M. Y. (2003). Predicting adolescents' intake of fruits and vegetables. *Journal of Nutrition Education and Behavior*, *35*(4), 170–178.

Pelters, B. & Wijma, B. (2016). Neither a sinner nor a saint: Health as a present-day religion in the age of healthism. *Social Theory & Health*, *14*(1), 129–148.

Piko, B. F. & Brassai, L. (2009). The role of individual and familial protective factors in adolescents' diet control. *Journal of Health Psychology*, *14*(6), 810–819.

Stathi, A. & Simey, P. (2007). Quality of life in the Fourth Age: exercise experiences of nursing home residents. *Journal of Aging and Physical Activity*, *15*(3), 272–286.

Steger, M. F., Fitch-Martin, A. R., Donnelly, J. & Rickard, K. M. (2015). Meaning in life and health: Proactive health orientation links meaning in life to health variables among American undergraduates. *Journal of Happiness Studies*, *16*(3), 583–597.

Takkinen, S., Suutama, T. & Ruoppila, I. (2001). More meaning by exercising? Physical activity as a predictor of a sense of meaning in life and of self-rated health and functioning in old age. *Journal of Aging and Physical Activity*, *9*(2), 128–141.

MORE ROUTINE!

Bond, M. J. & Feather, N. T. (1988). Some correlates of structure and purpose in the use of time. *Journal of Personality and Social Psychology*, 55, 321–329.

Bryan, C. J. & Center, J. S. (2015). Assessment and monitoring of astronaut behavioral health & psychological well-being following long-duration exploration missions.

Cotterill, S. (2010). Pre-performance routines in sport: Current understanding and future directions. *International Review of Sport and Exercise Psychology*, 3(2), 132–153.

De Ridder, D. & Gillebaart, M. (2017). Lessons learned from trait self-control in well-being: Making the case for routines and initiation as important components of trait self-control. *Health Psychology Review*, *11*(1), 89–99.

Heintzelman, S. J. & King, L. A. (2019). Routines and meaning in life. *Personality and Social Psychology Bulletin*, 45(5), 688–699.

Johnson, P. J. (2010). The roles of NASA, US astronauts and their families in long-duration missions. *Acta Astronautica*, 67(5–6), 561–571.

McKee-Ryan, F., Song, Z., Wanberg, C. R. & Kinicki, A. J. (2005). Psychological and physical well-being during unemployment: A meta-analytic study. *Journal of Applied Psychology*, *90*(1), 53–76.

Moriarty, P. H. & Wagner, L. D. (2004). Family rituals that provide meaning for single-parent families. *Journal of Family Nursing*, 10(2), 190–210.

Stavrova, O., Pronk, T. & Kokkoris, M. D. (2020). Finding meaning in self-control: The effect of self-control on the perception of meaning in life. *Self and Identity*, 19(2), 201–218.

Wooldredge, J. D. (1999). Inmate experiences and psychological well-being. *Criminal Justice and Behavior*, *26*(2), 235–250.

MAKE THINGS UP!

Axelson, T. (2008). Movies and meaning: Studying audience, fiction film and existential matters. *Participations: Journal of Audience and Reception Studies*, 5(1).

Halama, P. (2019). Compensatory function of conspiracy beliefs: Search for meaning in life moderates relationship between negative emotionality, stress and information control conspiracy beliefs (World Conference on Personality,
Kelemen, D., Rottman, J. & Seston, R. (2013). Professional physical scientists display tenacious teleological tendencies: Purpose-based reasoning as a cognitive default. *Journal of Experimental Psychology: general, 142*(4), 1074-1083.
Landau, M. J., Kosloff, S. & Schmeichel, B. J. (2011). Imbuing everyday actions with meaning in response to existential threat. *Self and Identity*, 10(1), 64-76.
Newheiser, A. K., Farias, M. & Tausch, N. (2011). The functional nature of conspiracy beliefs: Examining the underpinnings of belief in the Da Vinci Code conspiracy. *Personality and Individual Differences*, 51(8), 1007-1011.
Ramsay, J. E., Tong, E. M., Chowdhury, A. & Ho, M. H. R. (2019). Teleological explanation and positive emotion serially mediate the effect of religion on well-being. *Journal of Personality*, 87(3), 676- 689.

NARRATIZE YOUR LIFE!

Baumeister, R. F. & Vohs, K. D. (2002). The pursuit of meaningfulness in life. *Handbook of Positive Psychology*, 1, 608–618.
Cox, K. & McAdams, D. P. (2014). Meaning making during high and low point life story episodes predicts emotion regulation two years later: How the past informs the future. *Journal of Research in Personality*, 50, 66–70.
Habermas, T. & Bluck, S. (2000). Getting a life: the emergence of the life story in adolescence. *Psychological Bulletin*, 126(5), 748–769.
Heintzelman, S. J., Trent, J. & King, L. A. (2013). Encounters with objective coherence and the experience of meaning in life. *Psychological Science*, 24(6), 991–998.

Kay, A. C., Laurin, K., Fitzsimons, G. M. & Landau, M. J. (2014). A functional basis for structure-seeking: Exposure to structure promotes willingness to engage in motivated action. *Journal of Experimental Psychology: General*, 143(2), 486–491.

King, L. A., Heintzelman, S. J. & Ward, S. J. (2016). Beyond the search for meaning: A contemporary science of the experience of meaning in life. *Current Directions in Psychological Science*, 25(4), 211–216.

Korte, J., Westerhof, G. J. & Bohlmeijer, E. T. (2012). Mediating processes in an effective life-review intervention. *Psychology and Aging*, 27(4), 1172–1181.

Landau, M. J., Greenberg, J., Solomon, S., Pyszczynski, T. & Martens, A. (2006). Windows into nothingness: Terror management, meaninglessness, and negative reactions to modern art. *Journal of Personality and Social Psychology*, 90(6), 879–892.

Landmark, B. T., Strandmark, M. & Wahl, A. K. (2001). Living with newly diagnosed breast cancer – the meaning of existential issues: a qualitative study of 10 women with newly diagnosed breast cancer, based on grounded theory. *Cancer Nursing*, 24(3), 220–226.

Lee, V. (2008). The existential plight of cancer: meaning making as a concrete approach to the intangible search for meaning. *Supportive Care in Cancer*, 16(7), 779–785.

McAdams, D. P. (2001). The psychology of life stories. *Review of General Psychology*, 5(2), 100–122.

Proulx, T. & Heine, S. J. (2006). Death and black diamonds: Meaning, mortality, and the meaning maintenance model. *Psychological Inquiry*, 17(4), 309–318.

Routledge, C., Arndt, J., Sedikides, C. & Wildschut, T. (2008). A blast from the past: The terror management function of nostalgia. *Journal of Experimental Social Psychology*, 44(1), 132–140.

Steger, M. F. (2012). Making meaning in life. *Psychological Inquiry*, 23(4), 381–385.

Vaughan, S. M. & Kinnier, R. T. (1996). Psychological effects of a life review intervention for persons with HIV disease. *Journal of Counseling & Development*, 75(2), 115–123.

Westerhof, G. J., Bohlmeijer, E. T., Van Beljouw, I. M. & Pot, A. M. (2010). Improvement in personal meaning mediates the effects of a life review intervention on depressive symptoms in a randomized controlled trial. *The Gerontologist*, 50(4), 541–549.

Whiting, M. (2009). *"Is this my life?" Meaning and sense-making as key determinants of parents' experience when caring for children with disabilities, life-threatening/life-limiting illness or technology dependence* (Doctoral dissertation). London: London South Bank University.

Whitson, J. A. & Galinsky, A. D. (2008). Lacking control increases illusory pattern perception. *Science*, 322(5898), 115–117.

CONNECT!

Allan, B. A., Duffy, R. D. & Douglass, R. (2015). Meaning in life and work: A developmental perspective. *The Journal of Positive Psychology*, 10(4), 323–331.

Dechesne, M., Greenberg, J., Arndt, J. & Schimel, J. (2000). Terror management and the vicissitudes of sports fan affiliation: The effects of mortality salience on optimism and fan identification. *European Journal of Social Psychology*, 30(6), 813–835.

Eklund, M., Hermansson, A. & Håkansson, C. (2012). Meaning in life for people with schizophrenia: Does it include occupation? *Journal of Occupational Science*, 19(2), 93–105.

Grouden, M. E. & Jose, P. E. (2014). How do sources of meaning in life vary according to demographic factors? *New Zealand Journal of Psychology*, 43(3), 29–38.

Hicks, J. A. & King, L. A. (2007). Meaning in life and seeing the big picture: Positive affect and global focus. *Cognition and Emotion*, 21(7), 1577–1584.

Kiang, L. & Fuligni, A. J. (2010). Meaning in life as a mediator of ethnic identity and adjustment among adolescents from Latin, Asian, and European American backgrounds. *Journal of Youth and Adolescence*, 39(11), 1253–1264.

Lambert, N. M., Stillman, T. F., Hicks, J. A., Kamble, S., Baumeister, R. F. & Fincham, F. D. (2013). To belong is to matter: Sense of belonging enhances meaning in life. *Personality and Social Psychology Bulletin*, 39(11), 1418–1427.

Lambert, N. M., Stillman, T. F., Baumeister, R. F., Fincham, F. D., Hicks, J. A. & Graham, S. M. (2010). Family as a salient source of meaning in young adulthood. *The Journal of Positive Psychology*, *5*(5), 367–376.

Negru-Subtirica, O., Pop, E. I., Luyckx, K., Dezutter, J. & Steger, M. F. (2016). The meaningful identity: A longitudinal look at the interplay between identity and meaning in life in adolescence. *Developmental Psychology*, *52*(11), 1926–1936.

Patel, C. J., Ramgoon, S. & Paruk, Z. (2009). Exploring religion, race and gender as factors in the life satisfaction and religiosity of young South African adults. *South African Journal of Psychology*, *39*(3), 266–274.

Tiliouine, H. & Belgoumidi, A. (2009). An exploratory study of religiosity, meaning in life and subjective wellbeing in Muslim students from Algeria. *Applied Research in Quality of Life*, *4*(1), 109–127.

Steger, M. F. & Dik, B. J. (2009). If one is looking for meaning in life, does it help to find meaning in work? *Applied Psychology: Health and Well-Being*, *1*(3), 303–320.

Steger, M. F. & Frazier, P. (2005). Meaning in life: One link in the chain from religiousness to well-being. *Journal of Counseling Psychology*, *52*(4), 574–582.

Stillman, T. F., Baumeister, R. F., Lambert, N. M., Crescioni, A. W., DeWall, C. N. & Fincham, F. D. (2009). Alone and without purpose: Life loses meaning following social exclusion. *Journal of Experimental Social Psychology*, *45*(4), 686–694.

Tsay-Vogel, M. & Sanders, M. S. (2017). Fandom and the search for meaning: Examining communal involvement with popular media beyond pleasure. *Psychology of Popular Media Culture*, *6*(1), 32–47.

Van Orden, K. A., Bamonti, P. M., King, D. A. & Duberstein, P. R. (2012). Does perceived burdensomeness erode meaning in life among older adults? *Aging & Mental Health*, *16*(7), 855–860.

GET BETTER

Allred, S. L., Harrison, L. D. & O'connell, D. J. (2013). Self-efficacy: An important aspect of prison-based learning. *The Prison Journal*, *93*(2), 211–233.

Borowa, D., Kossakowska, M. M., Harmon, K. A. & Robitschek, C. (2018). Personal growth initiative's relation to life meaning and satisfaction in a Polish sample. *Current Psychology*, *39*, 1648–1660.

Machell, K. A., Kashdan, T. B., Short, J. L. & Nezlek, J. B. (2015). Relationships between meaning in life, social and achievement events, and positive and negative affect in daily life. *Journal of Personality*, *83*(3), 287–298.

Martin, L. A., Fogarty, G. J. & Albion, M. J. (2014). Changes in athletic identity and life satisfaction of elite athletes as a function of retirement status. *Journal of Applied Sport Psychology*, *26*(1), 96–110.

Meriläinen, M. (2014). Factors affecting study-related burnout among Finnish university students: teaching–learning environment, achievement motivation and the meaning of life. *Quality in Higher Education*, *20*(3), 309–329.

Nakamura, J. (2013). Pride and the experience of meaning in daily life. *The Journal of Positive Psychology*, *8*(6), 555–567.

O'Brien, E. & Kardas, M. (2016). The implicit meaning of (my) change. *Journal of Personality and Social Psychology*, *111*(6), 882–894.

Park, H. Y. (2017). Finding meaning through musical growth: Life histories of visually impaired musicians. *Musicae Scientiae*, *21*(4), 405–417.

Peterson, C., Park, N. & Seligman, M. E. (2005). Orientations to happiness and life satisfaction: The full life versus the empty life. *Journal of Happiness Studies*, *6*(1), 25–41.

Pike, A. (2015). *Prison-based transformative learning and its role in life after release* (Doctoral dissertation). The Open University.

Shin, J., Kim, M. S., Hwang, H. & Lee, B. Y. (2018). Effects of intrinsic motivation and informative feedback in service-learning on the development of college students' life purpose. *Journal of Moral Education*, *47*(2), 159–174.

Schueller, S. M. & Seligman, M. E. (2010). Pursuit of pleasure, engagement, and meaning: Relationships to subjective and objective measures of well-being. *The Journal of Positive Psychology*, *5*(4), 253–263.

Taubman-Ben-Ari, O., Shlomo, S. B. & Findler, L. (2012). Personal growth and meaning in life among first-time mothers and grandmothers. *Journal of Happiness Studies*, *13*(5), 801–820.

Triplett, K. N., Tedeschi, R. G., Cann, A., Calhoun, L. G. & Reeve, C. L. (2012). Posttraumatic growth, meaning in life, and life satisfaction in response to trauma. *Psychological Trauma: Theory, Research, Practice, and Policy*, 4(4), 400–410.

Vaksalla, A. & Hashimah, I. (2015). How hope, personal growth initiative and meaning in life predict work engagement among nurses in Malaysia private hospitals. *International Journal of Arts & Sciences*, 8(2), 321–378.

Vallerand, R. J. (2012). From motivation to passion: In search of the motivational processes involved in a meaningful life. *Canadian Psychology/Psychologie Canadienne*, 53(1), 42–52.

Vallerand, R. J. (2008). On the psychology of passion: In search of what makes people's lives most worth living. *Canadian Psychology/ Psychologie Canadienne*, 49(1), 1–13.

Yeager, D. S. & Bundick, M. J. (2009). The role of purposeful work goals in promoting meaning in life and in schoolwork during adolescence. *Journal of Adolescent Research*, 24(4), 423–452.

BE CREATIVE

Diedrich, J., Jauk, E., Silvia, P. J., Gredlein, J. M., Neubauer, A. C. & Benedek, M. (2018). Assessment of real-life creativity: The Inventory of Creative Activities and Achievements (ICAA). *Psychology of Aesthetics, Creativity, and the Arts*, 12(3), 304–316.

De Petrillo, L. & Winner, E. (2005). Does art improve mood? A test of a key assumption underlying art therapy. *Art Therapy*, 22(4), 205–212.

Fisher, B. J. & Specht, D. K. (1999). Successful aging and creativity in later life. *Journal of Aging Studies*, 13(4), 457–472.

Forgeard, M. J. (2013). Perceiving benefits after adversity: The relationship between self-reported posttraumatic growth and creativity. *Psychology of Aesthetics, Creativity, and the Arts*, 7(3), 245–264.

Griffin, A. (2016, 25 July). Binge watching TV can actually kill you, study finds. *Independent*. Hämtad 2020-10-23 från: https://www. independent. co.uk/news/science/binge-watching-tv-can-actually- kill-you-study-finds-a7155351.html

Griffin, G. A. (2002). Creativity and religious orientation: An interactional study of psychological well-being. *Dissertation Abstracts International: Section B: The Sciences and Engineering*, *63*(2– B), 1026.

Kaufman, J. C. (2018). Finding meaning with creativity in the past, present, and future. *Perspectives on Psychological Science*, *13*(6), 734– 749.

Liddle, J. L., Parkinson, L. & Sibbritt, D. W. (2013). Purpose and pleasure in late life: Conceptualising older women's participation in art and craft activities. *Journal of Aging Studies*, *27*(4), 330–338.

Metzl, E. S. (2009). The role of creative thinking in resilience after hurricane Katrina. *Psychology of Aesthetics, Creativity, and the Arts*, *3*(2), 112–123.

McCabe, M. & de Waal Malefyt, T. (2015). Creativity and cooking: Motherhood, agency and social change in everyday life. *Journal of Consumer Culture*, *15*(1), 48–65.

Moran, S. (2010). Changing the world: Tolerance and creativity aspirations among American youth. *High Ability Studies*, *21*(2), 117–132.

Moran, S. (2015). Adolescent aspirations for change: Creativity as a life purpose. *Asia Pacific Education Review*, *16*(2), 167–175.

Nell, W. (2014). Sources of life meaning among South African university students. *Journal of Psychology in Africa*, *24*(1), 82–91.

Niu, W. & Kaufman, J. C. (2013). Creativity of Chinese and American cultures: A synthetic analysis. *The Journal of Creative Behavior*, *47*(1), 77–87.

Pearce, E. (2017). Participants' perspectives on the social bonding and well-being effects of creative arts adult education classes. *Arts & Health*, *9*(1), 42–59.

Perach, R. & Wisman, A. (2019). Can creativity beat death? A review and evidence on the existential anxiety buffering functions of creative achievement. *The Journal of Creative Behavior*, *53*(2), 193–210.

Routledge, C., Arndt, J. & Sheldon, K. M. (2004). Task engagement after mortality salience: The effects of creativity, conformity and connectedness on worldview defence. *European Journal of Social Psychology*, *34*(4), 477–487.

Routledge, C., Arndt, J., Vess, M. & Sheldon, K. M. (2008). The life and death of creativity: The effects of mortality salience on self versus social-directed creative expression. *Motivation and Emotion*, *32*(4), 331–338.

Routledge, C. & Juhl, J. (2012). The creative spark of death: The effects of mortality salience and personal need for structure on creativity. *Motivation and Emotion*, *36*(4), 478–482.

Sherman, A. & Shavit, T. (2018). The thrill of creative effort at work: An empirical study on work, creative effort and well-being. *Journal of Happiness Studies*, *19*(7), 2049–2069.

Silvia, P. J., Beaty, R. E., Nusbaum, E. C., Eddington, K. M., Levin-Aspenson, H. & Kwapil, T. R. (2014). Everyday creativity in daily life: An experience-sampling study of "little c" creativity. *Psychology of Aesthetics, Creativity, and the Arts*, *8*(2), 183–188.

Simonton, D. K. (1989). The swan-song phenomenon: Last-works effects for 172 classical composers. *Psychology and Aging*, *4*(1), 42– 47.

Sligte, D. J., Nijstad, B. A. & De Dreu, C. K. (2013). Leaving a legacy neutralizes negative effects of death anxiety on creativity. *Personality and Social Psychology Bulletin*, *39*(9), 1152–1163.

Sloan, D. M., Marx, B. P., Epstein, E. M. & Dobbs, J. L. (2008). Expressive writing buffers against maladaptive rumination. *Emotion*, *8*(2), 302–306.

Stephenson, K. & Rosen, D. H. (2015). Haiku and healing: An empirical study of poetry writing as therapeutic and creative intervention. *Empirical Studies of the Arts*, *33*(1), 36–60.

Travagin, G., Margola, D. & Revenson, T. A. (2015). How effective are expressive writing interventions for adolescents? A meta-analytic review. *Clinical Psychology Review*, *36*, 42–55.

MAKE A DIFFERENCE

Allen, R. S., Hilgeman, M. M., Ege, M. A., Shuster Jr, J. L. & Burgio, L. D. (2008). Legacy activities as interventions approaching the end of life. *Journal of Palliative Medicine*, *11*(7), 1029–1038.

An, J. S. & Cooney, T. M. (2006). Psychological well-being in mid to late life: The role of generativity development and parent–child relationships across the lifespan. *International Journal of Behavioral Development*, *30*(5), 410–421.

Aubin, E. D. S. (2013). Generativity and the meaning of life. I: J. A. Hicks & C. Routledge (red.), *The experience of meaning in life. Classical perspectives, emerging themes, and controversies* (s. 241– 255). Dordrecht: Springer.

Bailey, A. W. & Fernando, I. K. (2012). Routine and project- based leisure, happiness, and meaning in life. *Journal of Leisure Research*, *44*(2), 139–154.

Cadrin, M. L. (2006). Music therapy legacy work in palliative care: Creating meaning at end of life/Le témoignage musicothérapeutique en soins palliatifs: Créer un sens en fin de vie. *Canadian Journal of Music Therapy*, *12*(1), 109.

Evangelista, L. S., Doering, L. & Dracup, K. (2003). Meaning and life purpose: the perspectives of post-transplant women. *Heart & Lung*, *32*(4), 250–257.

Franklin, F. C. & Cheung, M. (2017). Legacy interventions with patients with co-occurring disorders: legacy definitions, life satisfaction, and self-efficacy. *Substance Use & Misuse*, *52*(14), 1840–1849.

George, L. S. & Park, C. L. (2016). Meaning in life as comprehension, purpose, and mattering: Toward integration and new research questions. *Review of General Psychology*, *20*(3), 205–220.

Huta, V. & Zuroff, D. C. (2007). Examining mediators of the link between generativity and well-being. *Journal of Adult Development*, *14*(1–2), 47–52.

King, L. A., Heintzelman, S. J. & Ward, S. J. (2016). Beyond the search for meaning: A contemporary science of the experience of meaning in life. *Current Directions in Psychological Science*, *25*(4), 211–216.

Lips-Wiersma, M. & Morris, L. (2009). Discriminating between "meaningful work" and the "management of meaning." *Journal of Business Ethics*, *88*(3), 491–511.

Lucas, R. E., Clark, A. E., Georgellis, Y. & Diener, E. (2004). Unemployment alters the set point for life satisfaction. *Psychological Science*, *15*(1), 8–13.

Martela, F. & Steger, M. F. (2016). The three meanings of meaning in life: Distinguishing coherence, purpose, and significance. *The Journal of Positive Psychology*, *11*(5), 531–545.

McAdams, D. P., de St Aubin, E. D. & Logan, R. L. (1993). Generativity among young, midlife, and older adults. *Psychology and Aging*, *8*(2), 221–230.

Miller, A. D. & Rottinghaus, P. J. (2014). Career indecision, meaning in life, and anxiety: An existential framework. *Journal of Career Assessment*, *22*(2), 233–247.

Mousteri, V., Daly, M. & Delaney, L. (2018). The scarring effect of unemployment on psychological well-being across Europe. *Social Science Research*, *72*, 146169.

Ross, H. C. & Wolfe, S. E. (2016). Life after death: evidence of the Hoover Dam as a hero project that defends against mortality reminders. *Water History*, *8*(1), 3–21.

Simonton, D. K. (1989). The swan-song phenomenon: Last-works effects for 172 classical composers. *Psychology and Aging*, *4*(1), 42–47.

Steger, M. F., Kashdan, T. B. & Oishi, S. (2008). Being good by doing good: Daily eudaimonic activity and well-being. *Journal of Research in Personality*, *42*(1), 22–42.

Van Orden, K. A., Bamonti, P. M., King, D. A. & Duberstein, P. R. (2012). Does perceived burdensomeness erode meaning in life among older adults? *Aging & Mental Health*, *16*(7), 855–860.

Zhang, H., Sang, Z., Chan, D. K. S., Teng, F., Liu, M., Yu, S. & Tian, Y. (2016). Sources of meaning in life among Chinese university students. *Journal of Happiness Studies*, *17*(4), 1473–1492.

Zheng, X. & Wang, W. (2020). Whose time flies: meaning in life influences time awareness. *Journal of Adult Development*, 1–9.

Yeager, D. S. & Bundick, M. J. (2009). The role of purposeful work goals in promoting meaning in life and in schoolwork during adolescence. *Journal of Adolescent Research*, *24*(4), 423–452.

LIKE THE SITUATION!

Banerjee, K. & Bloom, P. (2015). "Everything happens for a reason": Children's beliefs about purpose in life events. *Child Development*, *86*(2), 503–518.

Bassett, J. F. & Going, S. B. (2012). A terror management analysis of perceived purpose: The effects of mortality salience on attributions for occurrences. *The Open Psychology Journal*, 5(1), 20–30.

Chan, W. C. H. & Chan, C. L. (2011). Acceptance of spousal death: The factor of time in bereaved older adults' search for meaning. *Death Studies*, 35(2), 147–162.

Datta, A., Aditya, C., Chakraborty, A., Das, P. & Mukhopadhyay, A. (2016). The potential utility of acceptance and commitment therapy (act) for reducing stress and improving well-being in cancer patients in Kolkata. *Journal of Cancer Education*, 31(4), 721–729.

Davis, C. G. & Morgan, M. S. (2008). Finding meaning, perceiving growth, and acceptance of tinnitus. *Rehabilitation Psychology*, 53(2), 128–138.

Fagbenro, D. A. & Olagundoye, H. F. (2019). Role of self-efficacy, life frustration, quality of health and meaning in life on suicidal ideation among adolescents: A Nigeria experience. *International Journal of Research*, 8(1), 15–25.

Flint, G. A., Gayton, W. F. & Ozmon, K. L. (1983). Relationship between life satisfaction and acceptance of death by elderly persons. *Psychological Reports*, 53(1), 290.

Landmark, B. T., Strandmark, M. & Wahl, A. K. (2001). Living with newly diagnosed breast cancer – the meaning of existential issues: a qualitative study of 10 women with newly diagnosed breast cancer, based on grounded theory. *Cancer Nursing*, 24(3), 220–226.

LaChapelle, D. L., Lavoie, S. & Boudreau, A. (2008). The meaning and process of pain acceptance. Perceptions of women living with arthritis and fibromyalgia. *Pain Research and Management*, 13(3), 201–210.

Lee, V. (2008). The existential plight of cancer: meaning making as a concrete approach to the intangible search for meaning. *Supportive Care in Cancer*, 16(7), 779–785.

Newcomb, M. D. & Harlow, L. L. (1986). Life events and substance use among adolescents: Mediating effects of perceived loss of control and meaninglessness in life. *Journal of Personality and Social Psychology*, 51(3), 564–577.

Paul, K. I., Vastamäki, J. & Moser, K. (2016). Frustration of life goals mediates the negative effect of unemployment on subjective well-being. *Journal of Happiness Studies*, 17(2), 447–462.

Whiting, M. (2009). *"Is this my life?" Meaning and sense-making as key determinants of parents' experience when caring for children with disabilities, life-threatening/life-limiting illness or technology dependence* (Doctoral dissertation). London: London South Bank University.

Wong, P. T. & Tomer, A. (2011). Beyond terror and denial: The positive psychology of death acceptance. *Death Studies*, 35(2), 99–106.

Zimmermann, F. F., Jordan, J. & Burrell, B. (2020). Coping with cancer mindfully: A feasibility study of a mindfulness intervention focused on acceptance and meaning in life for adults with advanced cancer. *European Journal of Oncology Nursing*, 44, 101715.

SEARCH (AND BE OPEN TO WHAT YOU FIND)

Brassai, L., Piko, B. F. & Steger, M. F. (2012). Existential attitudes and Eastern European adolescents' problem and health behaviors: Highlighting the role of the search for meaning in life. *The Psychological Record*, 62(4), 719–734.

Brassai, L., Piko, B. F. & Steger, M. F. (2015). A reason to stay healthy: The role of meaning in life in relation to physical activity and healthy eating among adolescents. *Journal of Health Psychology*, 20(5), 473–482.

Dursun, P., Steger, M. F., Bentele, C. & Schulenberg, S. E. (2016). Meaning and posttraumatic growth among survivors of the September 2013 Colorado floods. *Journal of Clinical Psychology*, 72(12), 1247–1263.

Newman, D. B., Nezlek, J. B. & Thrash, T. M. (2018). The dynamics of searching for meaning and presence of meaning in daily life. *Journal of Personality*, 86(3), 368–379.

Park, N., Park, M. & Peterson, C. (2010). When is the search for meaning related to life satisfaction? *Applied Psychology: Health and Well-Being*, 2(1), 1–13.

Pinquart, M. (2002). Creating and maintaining purpose in life in old age: A meta-analysis. *Ageing International*, 27(2), 90–114.

Peacock, E. J. & Reker, G. T. (1982). The Life Attitude Profile (LAP): Further evidence of reliability and empirical validity. *Canadian Journal of Behavioural Science/Revue canadienne des sciences du comportement*, 14(1), 92–95.

Reker, G. T., Peacock, E. J. & Wong, P. T. (1987). Meaning and purpose in life and well-being: A life-span perspective. *Journal of Gerontology*, *42*(1), 44–49.
Steger, M. F., Oishi, S. & Kashdan, T. B. (2009). Meaning in life across the life span: Levels and correlates of meaning in life from emerging adulthood to older adulthood. *The Journal of Positive Psychology*, *4*(1), 43–52.
Steger, M. F., Kawabata, Y., Shimai, S. & Otake, K. (2008). The meaningful life in Japan and the United States: Levels and correlates of meaning in life. *Journal of Research in Personality*, *42*(3), 660–678.
Steger, M. F., Kashdan, T. B., Sullivan, B. A. & Lorentz, D. (2008).
Understanding the search for meaning in life: Personality, cognitive style, and the dynamic between seeking and experiencing meaning. *Journal of Personality*, *76*(2), 199–228.
Steger, M. F., Frazier, P., Oishi, S. & Kaler, M. (2006). The meaning in life questionnaire: Assessing the presence of and search for meaning in life. *Journal of Counseling Psychology*, *53*(1), 80–93.
Shin, J. Y. & Steger, M. F. (2016). Supportive college environment for meaning searching and meaning in life among American college students. *Journal of College Student Development*, *57*(1), 18–31.
Steger, M. F., Mann, J. R., Michels, P. & Cooper, T. C. (2009). Meaning in life, anxiety, depression, and general health among smoking cessation patients. *Journal of Psychosomatic Research*, 67(4), 353–358.
Thrash, T. M., Elliot, A. J., Maruskin, L. A. & Cassidy, S. E. (2010). Inspiration and the promotion of well-being: Tests of causality and mediation. *Journal of Personality and Social Psychology*, *98*(3), 488– 506.
Vess, M., Routledge, C., Landau, M. J. & Arndt, J. (2009). The dynamics of death and meaning: The effects of death-relevant cognitions and personal need for structure on perceptions of meaning in life. *Journal of Personality and Social Psychology*, *97*(4), 728–744.

DON'T GIVE UP

Disabato, D. J., Goodman, F. R. & Kashdan, T. B. (2019). Is grit relevant to well-being and strengths? Evidence across the globe for separating perseverance of effort and consistency of interests. Journal of Personality, 87(2), 194–211.

Flinchbaugh, C., Luth, M. T. & Li, P. (2015). A challenge or a hindrance? Understanding the effects of stressors and thriving on life satisfaction. *International Journal of Stress Management, 22*(4), 323–345.

Kashdan, T. B. & Steger, M. F. (2007). Curiosity and pathways to well-being and meaning in life: Traits, states, and everyday behaviors. *Motivation and Emotion, 31*(3), 159–173.

Kleiman, E. M., Adams, L. M., Kashdan, T. B. & Riskind, J. H. (2013). Gratitude and grit indirectly reduce risk of suicidal ideations by enhancing meaning in life: Evidence for a mediated moderation model. *Journal of Research in Personality, 47*(5), 539–546.

WHAT CAN YOU DO TO FEEL A LITTLE MORE MEANING IN YOUR LIFE?

www.ingramcontent.com/pod-product-compliance
Lightning Source LLC
Chambersburg PA
CBHW031326230926
51848CB00001B/113
9789179653866